OLD NECTAR

A garden for all seasons

For Chris
Wishing you much happiness
designing beautiful gardens.
Una van der Spuy
author
2010

OLD NECTAR

A garden for all seasons

Una van der Spuy *Una van der Spuy*
(author)
2010

CONTENTS

6 Preface

9 **PART ONE:**
The garden at Old Nectar

13 The front garden

31 The rose garden

45 The pergola

61 The woodland garden

71 The bench garden

79 The back garden

91 The millstone terrace

100 **PART TWO:**
The Four Seasons

103 Spring

137 Summer

165 Autumn

187 Winter

205 Alien invader plants

205 Picture credits

206 Index

PREFACE

*Dedicated to the memory
of my late husband Kenneth Reid van der Spuy and to our three sons,
Anthony, Peter and David, and their families*

I started this book when I was 95 as the result of an accident.

While on holiday in Australia I was taking an early morning walk down a slope covered with dew-wet grass when I slipped – and crashed on to my back and broke four vertebrae. This was a disaster as I was due to fly back to South Africa the following day, but it was to be several weeks before I could make the journey.

On arrival home, where I live alone, I had to spend another six weeks lying flat on my back. It was then that I decided that I could entertain myself by writing a book about the garden.

For the past 55 years we have received groups of visitors to the garden during September and October to raise funds for various charities. Thousands of people have trod its paths and partaken of tea on the front stoep or in the garden, and for my staff and me hearing their complimentary remarks has been a delight. From letters and now e-mails received from visitors from many countries as well as from South Africans one realises that the memory of their visit has been impressive. Another incentive was the fact that the garden at Old Nectar is included in a recently published book, *1001 Gardens You Must See Before You Die*. This book describes what the authors consider to be the most beautiful gardens in the world.

Because I found it impossible to use a laptop while lying flat, the writing had to be by hand and even that was not easy.

Six months later, when I was able to get around the garden slowly on my crutches, my middle son, Peter, presented me with a digital camera on the eve of his return to Australia. What a joy and what fun I have had taking photographs of the garden to illustrate this book.

The photographs for my previous books had been with film cameras where the taking of close-up photographs involved mounting the camera on a tripod and, if there was wind or poor light, waiting for the wind to drop or the light to improve. It often took hours to get a good picture.

I was delighted with my new toy and set out with camera hanging from my wrist to make my way down to the top lawn. It was with some trepidation as it was a weekend and no staff were on duty to help should I fall. Although the digital camera is much easier to handle than my previous cameras I realised that I could not take photographs while balanced on crutches, so I dropped them on the front lawn, and then very slowly made my way around part of the garden taking photographs. At that stage pain limited my being on my feet to about 30 minutes at a time.

During the last 18 months I have taken about 2,000 photographs from which to make a selection for this book. I could not, however, have completed the book without the generous assistance of others.

Peter not only got me on to my feet by his gift of the camera but, on his visits, he continued to encourage and help in many different ways. It would, however, have been impossible to complete the project without the able assistance of Aileen Potgieter. She and her husband, Albert, spent most of their lives in Zimbabwe. They now live in a cottage at Old Nectar. Aileen has devoted endless hours deciphering my illegible handwriting, printing photographs from the laptop so that I could more easily decide which ones to use, helping with the selection and, last but not least, always being ready to take photographs, some of which I could not – either because the flowers were near ground level or too high, and a ladder was necessary to reach them.

I am also greatly indebted to Robert Thomson for his invaluable help. He too lives in a cottage at Old Nectar. Having finished the manuscript and sorted the illustrations into different categories, I was unable to work out how to align the captions with the photographs. Robert, who is an expert in the computer field, very kindly offered to put it all together. He finally printed it for me in the format of the finished book. This may sound simple but it took many hours of application as I continually made small changes to the text and to the selection of photographs.

Finally, when the book was ready to go to the publisher, I realised that it needed the attention of someone far better versed in the English language than I am, to read it through and make the necessary corrections. When I asked my old friend Dr Billy Trengove if he would do this, he readily consented and the book is all the better for his changes.

To make sure that the botanical names were correct I called upon my daughter-in-law Vivienne to check some of them on the web, and when it came to proofreading, my niece Ginn Fourie and dear friend Corinne Krige kindly stepped in to help after the designer, Jenny Young, had used her creative abilities to make it an attractive volume. Russell Martin of Jacana Media was ever helpful in seeing the book through all its stages. I am grateful to all of them for their help in the production of this book.

In concluding this preface, my hope is that the book will encourage readers to spend more time working in their gardens. The physical effort is undoubtedly good for the body and being outdoors attending to the needs of plants is relaxing and often inspiring, and good for the soul.

Una van der Spuy
Old Nectar
March 2009

There is an indefinable charm about the old Cape Dutch houses. The texture of the lime-plastered walls, the woodwork furrowed by age, the heavy shutters to the windows, and the fine entrance doors all contribute to a feeling of permanence. Old Nectar has, in addition, an exceptionally decorative front gable.

PART 1

THE GARDEN AT OLD NECTAR

The garden at Old Nectar is the only private garden in South Africa to have been designated a National Monument. This happened in 1967 at the same time as the Old Cape Dutch house which it surrounds. The citation reads: 'Old Nectar is architecturally one of the finest and best-known gabled houses of the old Cape type', and it was elsewhere described as 'The work of a master and perhaps the best example at the Cape of the late neo-classical gable on a small façade'. Being declared a National Monument does not mean that the state gives any financial support to the owners. It means only that the building or area so designated may not be altered in any significant way and that any proposed changes should be approved before being implemented.

In 1941 my husband and I acquired the property, then known as Glen Vashti, in the beautiful Jonkershoek Valley near Stellenbosch and 60 kilometres from Cape Town. It is a small subdivision of a large farm situated on the steep slope of the valley. The lower slopes of the mountains in the region are clothed in vineyards and the upper slopes are mostly rocky precipices. Between the two the ground is covered with indigenous vegetation – plants of many kinds including proteas. The climate in the region is what is known as 'Mediterranean', that is, it has rain in winter and dry summers.

The gracious old house was somewhat neglected and lacked all modern conveniences. There was no electricity, no indoor toilet and no bathroom. The war in Europe had started in 1939 and was to last for another four years during which time my husband would be fully engaged in military duties, so I, our three-year-old son, Anthony, and another son, Peter, born soon after our purchase of the property, would have his company at Old Nectar only four or five times and for only three or four days each time during the next four years.

'But why buy a property so far from military headquarters in Pretoria?' one might ask. There were two reasons. First, my husband was between assignments. For three years he had been Military Attaché representing the South African Defence Force, with an office in South Africa House, Trafalgar Square, London. In 1941 he was recalled to become Director-General of Technical Services with headquarters in Pretoria. Another and more cogent reason was that he had decided to retire as soon as the war ended and he wanted to retire to the town where he had been born and had spent the first six years of his life. As, in the intervening years he had not visited Stellenbosch, it seems that this was a kind of 'homing' instinct guiding him to end his life where he had begun it.

For me it was a challenge – to move from a well-equipped London home to a country property four kilometres from Stellenbosch and to deal with the problems of country life with few creature comforts. However, a lack of 'mod cons' was balanced against the fact that, as the war in Europe was entering an active phase, the comfortable London home might be bombed at any time and the rationing of food was such as to limit one to a dreary diet.

In 1941 Stellenbosch was a charming village with only one suburb. It had no tearoom, no restaurant and no ladies' hairdresser. There was, however, a builder and, within six months of arriving, our house acquired two bathrooms and two septic tanks to serve the toilets. Fortunately I knew how to design a septic tank as I had done a course on health management at the age of 19, during a university vacation. At the time one of my friends asked me, 'Why on earth are you doing such a dreary course?' and frowned at my reply: 'Who knows? Perhaps one day it will prove useful.' And barely ten years later it did. Unfortunately I knew nothing about gardening and the only subject I had not enjoyed at school was botany. I knew nobody in Stellenbosch from whom I could seek advice. There were no gardens worth the name in the only suburb of the town and, worse still, there was no South African gardening book available and no magazine devoted to gardening, for me to consult.

With the odds against me, I set to work with energy and enthusiasm, determined to convert the steep hillside between the house and the river below into a garden. The Old Nectar Garden is now well known locally and abroad. Each year visitors come from Europe, America and Japan, and it has been featured in British, French, German and Japanese books and periodicals.

It took five years to complete the garden, which covers about two acres. It is made up of seven gardens, each one distinct in style and character and most of them partially hidden from the others, so that moving from one area to the next reveals a completely different scene. Today when I look down from the house on to the terraced lawns, the rose garden, and, across the azaleas towards the woodland garden, it is difficult for me to picture how forbidding was the slope from the house to the river that confronted me on my arrival in the valley. In the 60 years since the garden was made I have changed little other than to introduce different plants.

The lovely old house with its wonderful front gable cried out for a setting worthy of it. But how was I, a 29-year-old who hardly knew a cabbage from a carnation, going to plan and then actually make the right kind of garden? The only thing I was certain about was that it had to be a romantic and peaceful garden in harmony with the house and the surroundings. How much should be formal in outline and how much informal? There should be a focal point, but where and what should it be?

Old Nectar has one of the most beautiful front gables of all the Cape Dutch houses still standing. The late Dr Mary Cook, who spent many years of her life studying this field of architecture, intimated to me that she was convinced that it was the work of Louis Thibault – a French architect who came to the Cape in 1783. He had studied under the chief architect to Louis XVI. Although the front gable is dated 1815 there is evidence of an earlier house that would have had a different gable. It was not unusual to change the façade of a house of that era.

Land in the area where the house stands had been granted to two freed slaves, Jan and Marquard van Ceylon in 1692. The surnames of slaves often indicated their country of origin and, in the Jonkershoek Valley, grants of land were made to other freed slaves bearing the surnames of van Bengale and van Angola. Jan van Ceylon planted 2,000 vines. His farming did not flourish and in 1712 his property was acquired by others.

The slaves at the Cape were from two different cultures, Eastern and African. About 50 per cent of them were from the countries with which the Dutch East India Company was then trading: Indonesia, southern India and Ceylon (Sri Lanka). This Dutch business enterprise had established a small settlement at the Cape soon after 1652 to provide fresh food for their sailing ships, which took six months from Holland to Indonesia. Not all of these Eastern people brought to the Cape were slaves. Some were political prisoners. There is, for example, a record of two sons of a one-time Emperor of Java sent to the Cape because of their political activities in their home country. Of the slaves of African origin most of them were from Mauritius, Madagascar or Mozambique.

The majority of the landowners who built the old Cape Dutch homes were from Holland but there were also citizens of France, refugees who had fled religious persecution in their own country in 1688, and there was a small number of German origin. Most of the craftsmen who actually did the work we so admire today were the slaves from the East.

Unfortunately there are few records of the problems the owners of land might have had with the builders and in obtaining the materials required for the building operations. The bricks were made on the premises and not fired to make them hard. No cement was available and these soft bricks are held together by layers of clay soil set between them, with a final coating of lime plaster.

All the buildings of that period were thatched. The roof of Old Nectar was thatched but is now corrugated iron painted ash-grey. There is no record of when this was done. It could have been late in the 19th century when a fire raged in Stellenbosch and many houses were damaged or destroyed. The ceilings and floors are of wide boards of yellowwood probably brought from Knysna (an area of natural forests 400 kilometres east of Cape Town) and from there by ox or mule wagon. This was a tremendous undertaking as some of the flooring boards are 30 cm wide, 6 cm thick and 8 m long and therefore extremely heavy. On top of the ceiling is a layer of bricks covered by a thin layer of earth. This was to prevent the ceiling catching alight and is known as a *brandsolder*. It was a practical idea adopted by the owners of most of the homes of that period to insulate the wooden ceiling.

During the centuries the name of the property changed several times. The name Nektar was given to it in 1813 but was changed in 1920, again in 1935 and again by us in 1941. As another small property carved out of the large farm had been named Mount Nectar, we called our property Old Nectar. Nektar was an unusual name to give a farm in the early 19th century. They usually had Dutch or French names such as Weltevreden or La Rochelle.

We think that the two urns – each with its ladle – at the top of the gable might be an indication that the farm was a wine farm, the urns to contain nectar – in mythology, the drink of the gods. It says a great deal for the builders that, during the years since the house was erected, it has endured with little by way of repairs. The walls have not developed cracks nor does the roof leak.

When I arrived at Old Nectar I knew the names of only a few trees and shrubs and what they looked like, and of these few I didn't know their final height and spread. The difficulties overwhelmed me for a time until I found, in a second-hand bookshop, a copy of a book by an Australian author called Brunning. This is not a glamorous book full of colour pictures. It was published long before the days of colour photography. There are few illustrations and the paper on which it is printed is of poor quality, but the author's wide knowledge and clear presentation of every aspect of gardening made it a most useful reference work.

In those days nurseries produced printed catalogues naming and describing the plants they propagated. Gardeners who lived nearby would make their choice of plants by visiting them; those far from a nursery would post an order for delivery by rail to the station nearest their home. I wrote letters to nurseries all over the country and studied their catalogues in the evening after I had put the children to bed. I lived alone and spent endless hours making notes – literally burning the midnight oil and, when oil (paraffin) ran out, the flickering candle.

A main electric cable was not extended into the Jonkershoek Valley until after the end of the war – five years later. It could have been done in the first year after my arrival. I had asked the Electricity Supply Commission what they required of the residents to justify bringing a cable into the valley. Their reply was £30 per month. Easy, thought I. The neighbours will all be overjoyed. I visited them – the Department of Forestry, the Trout Hatchery and their staff, and five neighbouring farmers. The farmers reply in general was: 'We get up when it's light and go to bed when it's dark. We don't need electricity.' The Forestry and Fishing departments would pay only £5 per month, and with my £5 we were far short of the £30 per month required. In autumn of the following year it occurred to me that, if I rode to the neighbouring farms on horseback rather than arriving again by car, the suggestion of using electricity in their homes might be more positively received. It worked. They were all prepared to join the scheme but, alas, by then it was impossible to import the necessary cable as there was little shipping between England and South Africa.

Development came to a halt after a few months as I suddenly found myself with no assistance outdoors and in the house. What was worse, there was nobody to milk the two cows or to feed and groom the two mules and two horses we had taken over with the property. This was a crisis as the cows had to be milked twice a day. I endeavoured to do the task myself but soon realised that persuading a cow to yield its milk was an art that required practice. I tried every kind of finger manoeuvre but not a drop emerged. The cow turned its head and eyes towards me with a supercilious stare; a heave of its body, followed by a kick, and I was unseated. Dignity and determination lost, I phoned a neighbour who immediately sent one of his staff to help. It was my first labour problem and, had I known then that this kind of problem would be part of my life at Old Nectar, I might have decided then and there that life in the country was not for me.

At that time it was difficult to find staff to help with the development of the garden. Many coloured men had joined the armed forces and there were very few black people living or working in the Western Cape then. Fortunately, in a few weeks the problem was solved. I was to get four Italian prisoners of war who wished to work on farms. The previous year, in one of the many battles that raged in North Africa, a large force of the Italian army had surrendered and the British government, being short of food for their own population, had asked the South African government to house and feed them. A huge area of buildings at Zonderwater, near Pretoria, was provided for them and those who elected to work on farms were allowed to do so.

The men, who arrived by train under escort at Stellenbosch, were four in number. Giuseppe, aged 64, bald-headed with a frill of grey hair around the ears. He said he had been a chef on an Italian passenger liner, but it turned out that even his compatriots complained about the food he served them. He was a crafty man who always had a reason for not helping. The next in age was Borraro, a carpenter, aged 35. He did not excel at carpentry and was not keen on doing any other kind of work. Then there was Gatti – a sturdily built, 19-year-old farmer's son with little education but a lot of drive, who was to remain on the property until the war ended and who later returned and started making ice-cream in a backroom in Cape Town. Within ten years he was a wealthy man with a farm and an ice-cream factory, Gattis, which made excellent ice-cream, much in demand. The fourth man was Dante, who knew something of brick-laying and helped in various other ways to make the garden. Unfortunately there wasn't a gardener amongst them but at least I now had four pairs of hands to do what had to be done. The trouble was that, although I had a plethora of ideas, I still did not really know exactly what the ideas would produce visually. Obviously lawns in front of the house would come first.

And so we started … to move a mountain manually in order to create the garden.

PART 1

THE FRONT GARDEN

I decided against having a central path leading from the front steps as, to my mind, there should be plain lawn as the foreground to the exceptionally decorative gable.

To give the area a feeling of stability the steeply sloping ground would have to be terraced. No easy task before the days of bulldozers. Tons and tons of soil were moved in those first five years by pickaxe, shovel, wheelbarrow and muscle power.

When the first two terraces were completed, the idea of making a swimming pool on the third one crept into my thoughts. Nowadays one phones a contractor and, hey presto, the pool is installed. There were no swimming pools in Stellenbosch and probably none in Cape Town either at that time. I had no guide lines and there were no books on 'How to design and make a swimming pool'. By this time summer had come. It was extremely hot and the swimming pool dream had to be tackled at once.

I drew up a plan, discussed it with Dante, and we worked out how many bricks to order and how much cement to buy. The movement of more soil now took place to ensure that the top of the pool would be on the same level as the lawn that would in time surround it. The next task was the laying of the bricks. At that time I knew little about building and deferred to Dante, who decided to make the walls first and the floor last. I was not altogether happy about this process on logical grounds – surely a foundation should come first – and also because I'd heard that prisoners of war going out to work would

RIGHT: *The house, as the sun rises over the mountain behind.*

sabotage wherever they could. I therefore asked the only building contractor in the area to call and advise me. It was as I thought. Not only should the floor be laid first but there should be reinforcing rods within the concrete floor 60 cm apart, extending up into the walls to hold it all together. So, the walls, which by this time were almost a metre high, had to be pulled down whilst I drove to a builder's yard in Cape Town to procure reinforcing rods.

After problems of various kinds the pool was completed and filled. In my ignorance I had planned a pool far larger than it need have been. It says a lot for Dante's workmanship that it has never cracked nor leaked. Should I wake up one morning and find it empty it will be my own fault because I planted two Lombardy poplars only two metres from the edge of the pool. What did I know about the roots of trees? Nothing; and Leslie Brunning's gardening book, *The Australian Gardener*, did not mention that poplars have wide-spreading roots and should not be planted within 15 metres of a building. The poplars are now 37 metres tall with huge roots. Since then I have read hundreds of books on gardening and on trees but never found one that mentioned the nature of their roots.

The decision to plant two Lombardy poplars to make a focal point to the garden was due to the fact that in 1937 I had travelled through Italy and been much impressed by these poplars when visiting the Lombardy region.

Next came the planting of the lawn. From friendly farmers I got roots of kikuyu grass to plant over the whole area and after three months there was a vivid green lawn ready to be mown. What an accomplishment, I thought, and what a joy after all the worries about the pool-building and the task of making and levelling the terraces. The next problem was finding a lawnmower. Only two firms in Cape Town dealt in them and they had none in stock. All lawnmowers were imported and, because at that time so many ships were being sunk by German submarines, nobody knew when the next shipment would reach our shores. By advertising I finally managed to get a second-hand manual mower – the only type available in those days.

One of the most magnificent of trees for large gardens is the copper beech. Finding a plant for my garden took years, and I was delighted when about 50 years ago I discovered a small nursery able to supply one. I planted it next to the stream so that as the roots spread they would find water. At that time I did not know that as it grew its strong spreading roots would inhibit the growth of other plants, even the lawn, and that they too might crack the wall of the swimming pool only three metres from its trunk. I keep my fingers crossed!

The oldest copper beech I have seen in our country is well over a hundred years old and the oldest about which I have heard of more or less the same age is on a farm in the Maclear district of the Drakensberg mountain region. How enterprising were gardeners and nurserymen of that period, for they had to import most of the trees from Europe. The ships of that time would have taken a minimum of four weeks to make the voyage from England to the port of Durban and then, before the days of a train service and before cars, the young plants would have had a four-to-five-day journey by ox wagon. Would that we had such enterprising gardeners and nurserymen today, and that the many wonderful decorative trees and shrubs available three to four generations ago were still on nursery lists.

On the same level as the top terrace right next to the slave bell was an unattractive old irrigation pond. Improve its appearance and let it become a special feature, I thought.

We enhanced its muddy bank by making a stone wall and a brick pathway around it and planted ground covers about its perimeter to form a colourful curtain of greenery and flowers to embellish the bank. The area between the pond and the stables needed to be hidden from view, so there I planted ornamental trees and shrubs. The group includes a flowering cherry with pale green flowers, one of the lovely pinky-mauve, winter-flowering magnolias, a variegated maple from the United States, *Acer negundo* 'Variegatum', whose ivory-marked green leaves make a charming background to the old bell-tower, and the tree known as Australian frangipani (hymenosporum). The lower planting includes the rose Crepuscule, the sweetly scented white jasmine, honeysuckle and philadelphus, whose graceful stems of white flowers bring fragrance to the air after the jasmine is over and before the Australian frangipani produces its sweetly scented flowers.

Scent is an essential in any garden. It introduces a subtle dimension that one remembers long after one has passed by. In addition to scented flowers there are the plants with scented leaves. I have planted rosemary, lavender, lemon-scented balm and verbena in the areas where there are no plants with scented flowers, and I encourage those who walk by to pick a twig from them in passing. It adds to one's enjoyment and keeps the plants from growing too high and wide.

It is interesting to note how many scented flowers are white, indicating perhaps that scent is necessary to attract the insects that pollinate them. However, of the roses I know, those with the most pervasive scent are red.

One of the main attractions of this round pond is the reflections revealed on its dark surface. Each step of a walk around it mirrors something different: the slave bell, the gable of the house, trees and the mountain. I walk around it most evenings just after sunset when the reflections are sharp and crisp.

The water from the pond cascades down two metres to run into two small pools we made on the level of the second terrace. Here we planted water-side plants from different countries – the dramatic gunnera from the cold area of Peru is a deciduous plant. Its new leaves emerge crinkled, the size of a dinner plate, and unfold and enlarge to measure a metre or more across when fully grown. On the other side of the stream is the mop-headed papyrus from Egypt. It is decorative, but in a small garden it should be grown in a container to restrict the spread of its roots. We remove half of them every year to keep them within bounds.

RIGHT: *The Lombardy poplars and copper beech make a splendid picture in this reflection.*

LEFT *Reflections: The Norfolk Island pine and Australian frangipani and the mountain opposite.*
RIGHT *The slave bell and surrounding curtains of ground covers ornamenting the wall of the pond.*

This view of the front garden is towards the town of Stellenbosch, four kilometres away. The two white urns flanking the steps down to the next terrace and the golden conifer and shaped golden privet add colour to the scene all year through. By leading the eye, the low hedges are an invitation to explore what is hidden from view.

ABOVE: *On the one side of the top terrace the lawn is bordered by plants with colourful foliage for year-round effect. The gold-tinged leaves are golden privet and the bronze is polygonum – a ground cover that develops into a rounded form very quickly. Variegated periwinkle in the foreground and the silvery leaves of dusty miller in the background enhance the scene.*

OPPOSITE: *An ugly old farm pond that irrigated an ancient orchard lower down the slope was transformed into a special feature. A brick-and-stone wall and walkway replaced the muddy bank and ground covers were planted around the perimeter to make cascading curtains of colour. Water lilies now add lustre to its surface and the reflections change constantly all day long.*

ABOVE: *The steps are unique inasmuch as they lead down both sides as well as the front. Because they appeared to be harsh and austere, we planted small ground covers here and there to soften their outline. The slave bell, like the steps, has many a tale to tell.*

LEFT: *From the grooves worn in the side steps one concludes that these were used more often than the stately but forbidding front ones. The white daisies of erigeron and the charming blue flowers of the indigenous geranium decorate the steps. Geraniums have five petals evenly arranged in a bowl shape (see page 116) whereas the five petals of pelargoniums are irregular in their arrangement.*

ABOVE: *The most difficult part of the garden is in front of the wall of the stoep, the reason being that it is in deep shade until midday and then gets the intense summer sun until sunset. No plants like such conditions. The ground cover is creeping Jenny, with trimmed golden privet and variegated abutilon as a contrast to the colour of the parapet walls. The elegant rounded wall is the backrest of a rounded bench on the stoep.*

RIGHT: *In a pot on the stoep is an unusual plant with delightful clusters of tiny grey leaves and prettily marked brick-red flowers. The name of this trailing lotus is* Lotus berthelotii.

LEFT: *Below the old pond the water flows through two small pools. The stream with its three waterfalls makes a delightful border to the front garden and separates it from the rose garden. The sides of the stream are embellished with low-growing plants, ground covers and dwarf roses. The large leaves and conical flowers are of the plant gunnera.*

RIGHT: *From the water feature one has a view framed by two snowballs across the top two terraces of the front garden. Note how pleasing in the foreground is the contrast in colour of the silver leaves of lamb's ear, the gold of a privet and the bronze of berberis.*

LEFT: *A narrow stone-and-brick path leads down the slope by the side of the pools. Here again colour is provided by the leaves of perennial plants – the bronze polygonum and golden privet, both drought- and frost-resistant plants.*

RIGHT: *Columbines enjoy the shade beside the water. Their fernlike foliage adds charm to the area after the flowers fade.*

ABOVE: *A small group of azaleas nestling in the shade on one side of the front steps highlights that area in spring.*

RIGHT: *Azaleas bring sparkle to different areas near the house. This lovely one has flowers with long stamens which make it all the more attractive.*

OPPOSITE: *This delightful show of colour greets one on arrival at the parking place near the house. These azaleas thrive with little attention other than watering at ground level through a drip system. When they are not in flower, the leaves continue to make a verdant screen between the car park and the garden. Botanically azaleas have now become rhododendrons, but I feel that generations to come will still use the term azaleas.*

26

ABOVE: *The yellow azalea belongs to a group that is deciduous. When its stems, which have been bare of leaves all winter, become covered with their golden flowers, it is a glorious sight. The colourful ground cover in its shade is a lamium.*

LEFT: *In the background a giant ageratum nestles in the shade of a burgundy-coloured prunus, and azaleas highlight the foreground.*

OPPOSITE LEFT: *Here a pale-pink pelargonium flaunts its beauty by climbing into an azalea.*

ABOVE: *The water in the swimming pool on the bottom terrace has a dark glow which harmonises with its surroundings and reveals different reflections throughout the day.*

LEFT: *We planted camellias for winter colour in all areas of the garden. Two of them near the house are special inasmuch as I planted them on the birth of my first two granddaughters – Martine, who lives in Sydney, Australia, is white and pink ... and Tonia, who lives in the United States, is snow-white. In other parts of the garden there are trees and shrubs named for other members of the family.*

The lawn on the middle terrace narrows to pass between two curved borders of shrubs to form a path from the front garden to the rose garden. Through the different gardens I laid emphasis on curves rather than straight lines. Note how the colours of the leaves of shrubs and trees highlight this scene. In the foreground to the bell arch is a trimmed golden conifer; on the same level in front is a bronze polygonum. American maples (Acer negundo 'Variegatum') form the background to the bell. On a lower level are a golden elder and a burgundy-coloured prunus with golden privets in the foreground.

PART 1

THE ROSE GARDEN

I decided that there had to be a formal rose garden on the adjoining slope so there followed more pickaxe/shovel/muscle power/wheelbarrow work – moving four metres from the top of the slope to put on the lower part of the slope. What is now done by an earthmover in a day took the Italian prisoners of war about four months to complete. I had set my heart on a circular rose garden rather than a square or rectangular one, which would not suit the site or the surroundings. And so it evolved – a perfect circle 25 metres in diameter, with a small round lawn in the middle surrounded by eight wedge-shaped beds each planted with 45 rose plants less than a metre apart.

Before the area was planted it was trenched to a width and depth of 60 cm and old stable (horse) manure mixed with the soil returned to the trenches. I wanted these plants to flourish for a long time and I succeeded in my objective as in three of the beds there still grow and flower well three of the cultivars I planted 63 years ago, namely Etoile de Hollande, Otto Thilow and Crimson Glory. These were then the most popular roses in the USA and England. By this time I had joined the American and British rose societies and was learning a great deal from their journals. In the other five beds the plants are now 30 to 40 years old.

The rose garden, which is on a much lower level than the house, makes a wonderful picture as seen from the front stoep, and is colourful from October to July. But it is only after the roses are pruned that one can appreciate the outline of the rose garden. A rose garden has to have a background so that when the roses are not in flower that area remains attractive. It is surrounded by decorative trees and shrubs. Coming down the steps from the round pond one has, on the left, the rich bronze leaves of the prunus. There are two cultivars worth a place in small and large gardens: *Prunus cerasifera* 'Nigra' and 'Pissardii'. It is interesting to note that the latter-named cultivar derives from a sport found sometime before 1880 in the garden of the Shah of Persia, by his French gardener, M. Pissard.

OPPOSITE: *The rose garden is a constant source of pleasure from the moment I open the front door of the house in the morning until I close it in the evening, for it lies on a much lower level than the house and one therefore has an exceptional view looking down on it. It is made up of eight wedge-shaped beds, and in each one are roses of the same colour. This creates a more harmonious scene than having mixed colours in the beds. The silver leaves of snow-in-summer provide a narrow edging to the beds that defines their borders in an attractive fashion. The Norfolk Island pine is flanked on the right by an Australian frangipani and on the left by an American maple.*

At one's feet is a short hedge of berberis with leaves the same colour as the prunus and, near it, for colourful contrast, is a group of dusty miller with prettily indented silver foliage. As it tends to become bedraggled with age, we remove the old plants every second year and put in new ones that we have made from cuttings. They root very easily. This is one of the best plants to highlight the garden with silver, and silver is a splendid foil to all other colours. Between the rich bronze of the berberis and the prunus, the silvery leaves of a gazania shine out. Such a useful ground-cover plant this, for impossibly rugged places, as once established it rarely needs to be watered. Here there are also easy-to-grow perennials such as agapanthus, day lily and pineapple flower, which require little water and which fill in a lot of space with their attractive foliage almost all the year through. Gardening should be fun and not hard work, so I go for plants with decorative foliage that keep growing without much care.

On the bank on the left of the circle grows an enthusiastic plant that, during much of the year, is a focal point from almost any part of the garden. It is the golden form of the common elderberry (sambucus). It loses its leaves in winter but, come spring, long stems of gold-tinged leaves emerge, and it commands the attention of all who pass by. We cut it back by a third each year and occasionally we dig up side roots when it grows too wide. It is not under any watering system and doesn't flinch at being without water during the dry months. In a small garden it should be planted in a container sunk in the ground to restrict its spread.

ABOVE LEFT: *In mid-winter, after the roses have been pruned, the rose garden still remains attractive because of its clearly delineated form emphasised by the brick paths. The tree, Norfolk Island pine, makes a wonderful focal point to the scene.*

LEFT: *This bed is of my favourite rose, Crimson Glory, loved for several reasons. The plant is of a good shape – round and bushy – not tall and lanky; it produces an abundance of blooms of a rich deep crimson shade; the buds are beautiful in shape and open to sculptured flowers – lovely on the bush and enchanting when arranged with short stems in a large flat bowl on a table so that one can look down on them. To add to these attributes, it has the best scent of all the roses I know. The scent pervades the areas where they grow and indoors, in an arrangement.*

Other plants on that dry bank are privet, nandina and plumbago. They are cut back each year to prevent them from becoming a tangle. It sounds like hard work but I find trimming and cutting back the fast-growing shrubs a fun task. My staff love doing it and sometimes annoy me by doing it at the wrong time of the year, which means that the plants fail to flower the following season.

The trimming of shrubs, which in most cases should be done every year to keep them from becoming too large and untidy, is best done soon after their flowering, or at least six months before the next flowering is due. Plumbago and abelia, which flower in summer, should be cut back between April and June. Cape may (spiraea), which flowers in late winter and early spring, should be cut back between November and January. If one does the cutting as soon as flowering is over, one is not likely to make a mistake. How much to cut back depends on the rate of growth of the plant and its size. A fast-growing one can be trimmed down to knee height. One needs to keep shrubs within the confines of the space they have been allocated in the garden.

One of the two focal points of the whole garden as seen from the house is the proud and stately Norfolk Island pine. This is a very special tree from a sentimental point of view. When I planted it I had never seen even a picture of one, but the description in the nursery catalogue led me to believe that it was the best of all the evergreen trees, and I wanted it to be a memorial to my husband. I planted it in the fifth year of the war. Those of us who had husbands on military service wondered

ABOVE RIGHT: *This lovely rose is named Maria Callas after the famous operatic singer. Flamboyant and beautiful, it demands admiration from all who pass by.*

RIGHT: *A metal ornament, made by Italian prisoners of war in their camp near Pretoria, graces the eastern edge of the rose garden. In spring nasturtiums frolic around its base and attempt to climb its sides. It is a good memorial to the years 1942–45 when four or five prisoners of war worked with me to make the garden. I am deeply aware of the debt I owe them, not only for the results of their hard work but also because they taught me to speak their language. It is not surprising that the first word I learned was* letama, *which means manure!*

whether we would ever see them again. He was one of the fortunate ones, for he participated in and survived two world wars and two years in a criminal jail in Russia (1918–20) during the Bolshevik Revolution, to die peacefully at home soon after his 99th birthday. By then his tree was nearly 50 years old and already dominated the scene. We made a simple curved brick bench at the foot of his tree and attached to it a remembrance plaque.

> This Tree was planted in 1944 by Una as a tribute to
> Kenneth Reid van der Spuy C.B.E., M.C. 1892–1991
> Who served in the R.F.C., R.A.F., S.A.A.F.
> Remembered for his courage and devotion to duty;
> His love of adventure and of life;
> His appreciation of nature and his sense of humour.

I am convinced that a sense of humour increases one's life span. He remained slender all his life and mentally and physically active. He wrote his autobiography when he was 73 and a record of Stellenbosch, which required a good deal of research, when he was 85. He also wrote poetry from time to time.

ABOVE LEFT: *This is the view towards the dry, unwatered slope above the rose garden as one approaches it from the front garden. The foreground plant is a bronze berberis; it is backed by the silver leaves of dusty miller. On the dry bank grow plum-coloured prunus, golden elder, privet, plumbago, nandina, and the large-leaf privet as a tall hedge. It makes a pretty evergreen shade tree for regions where water is in short supply.*

LEFT: *The memorial garden we made for my husband is under the Norfolk Island pine, which was planted for him 50 years before he died. I purposely repeated the circular shape of the rose garden in the design – a small circular paved area with a bench making an arc of a circle and two rounded golden privets standing sentinel on either side of the approach path. Such repetition of a form or shape makes a harmonious picture.*

OPPOSITE: *From the memorial garden one has a splendid view across the rose garden to the front façade of the house that my husband so dearly loved, with its grand mountain background. It is an inspiring and peaceful scene.*

ABOVE: *Above the rose garden is a group of ornamental trees, which includes a Japanese cherry with pale-green flowers.*

RIGHT: *In early winter the main colours on the edge of the rose garden are the flame leaves of a Japanese maple contrasted with the gold-tinged ones of neighbouring plants – a conifer and a coprosma.*

OPPOSITE: *This magnolia (M. soulangeana) is one of eight I planted about 50 years ago to spread colour across the garden in winter. It adds beauty to the rose garden when the roses are dormant.*

ABOVE: *Before the roses start flowering in October the bank behind the old pond and above the rose garden glows with colour – the brilliant white of Cape may, giant ageratum with pale amethyst flowers, the richly coloured leaves of a prunus, and the golden ones of an elder.*

OPPOSITE PAGE:

TOP LEFT: *Maria Callas is a rounded plant which makes a dramatic show when it produces its rich carmine blooms on strong stems.*

BOTTOM LEFT: *This lovely rose of a deep gold colour bears the name South Africa. It is a sturdy grower of good form.*

TOP RIGHT: *Duet is fairly tall and stately in growth the better to display its pretty flowers with frilly petals darker pink on one side than the other.*

BOTTOM RIGHT: *Una van der Spuy is a tall grower with ivory buds flushed with palest pink opening to a rounded bloom with petals that fold back.*

39

ABOVE: *Johannesburg Sun* has long pointed buds that open to a delightful flower of a rich gold colour with a soft fragrance. It is a vigorous grower.

ABOVE LEFT: *Angel Bells* forms a bush of moderate size which carries its exquisite flowers of ivory outlined with deep pink on firm stems with glossy leaves throughout the growing months.

LEFT: *Golden Monica* has lovely pointed buds of a golden tone that develop into blooms with wide-preading petals. Its long stems make this a good cut flower.

OPPOSITE: *Crimson Glory* – my favourite rose already described.

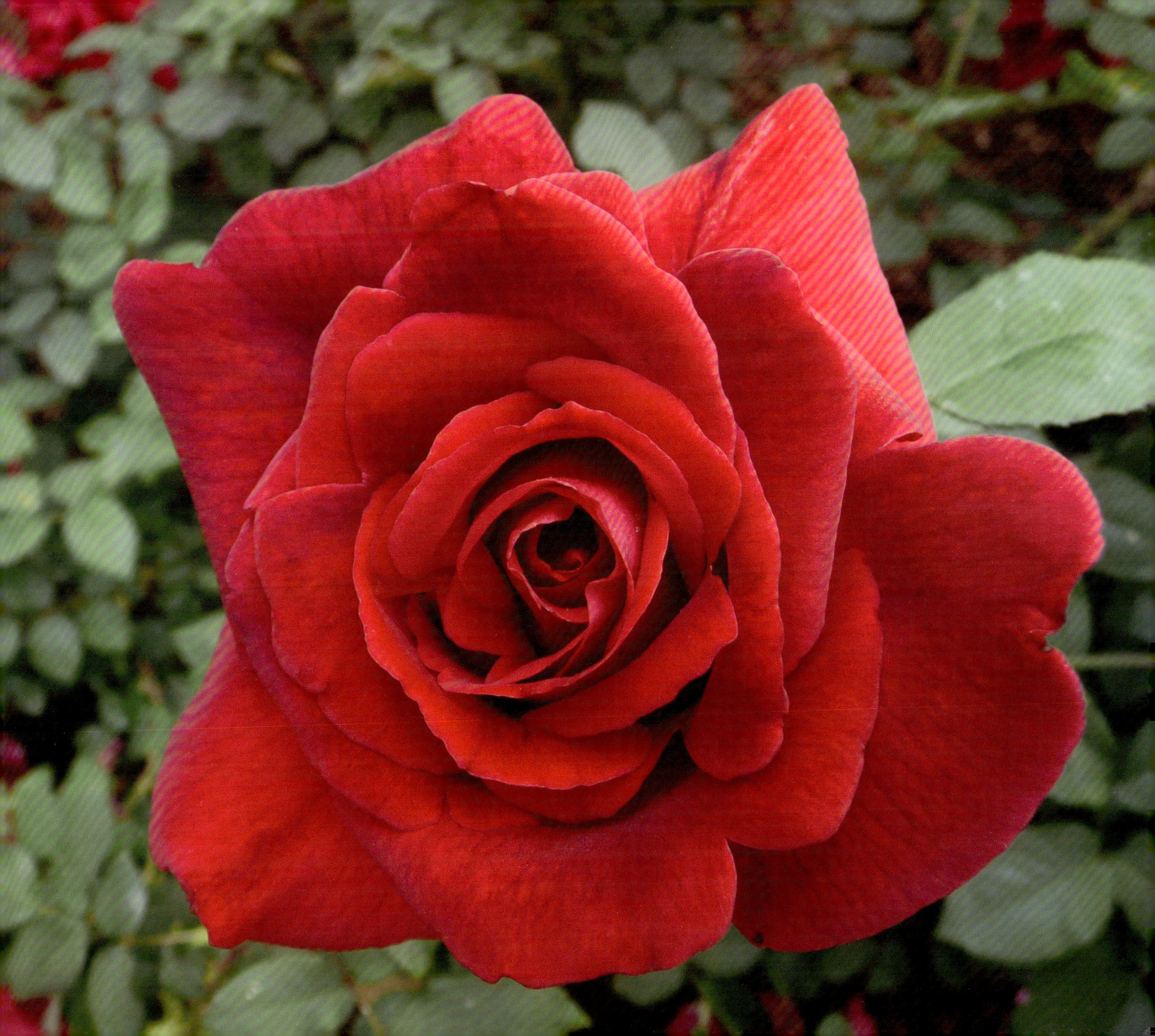

ABOVE: *Peace is a renowned rose introduced 60 years ago. It has beautifully shaped buds that open to a lovely, firm flower with yellow petals edged with pink.*

ABOVE LEFT: *Duftwolke, which translates into 'fragrant cloud', has spectacular scented flowers of an arresting flame shade on long stems. It is a sturdy plant.*

LEFT: *Queen Elizabeth is a strong, tall-growing plant that bears a profusion of lovely blooms of blush pink on long stems. Good in the garden and for arrangements.*

OPPOSITE: *Casanova produces large, lightly fragrant flowers on long stems. It is a vigorous plant with good foliage.*

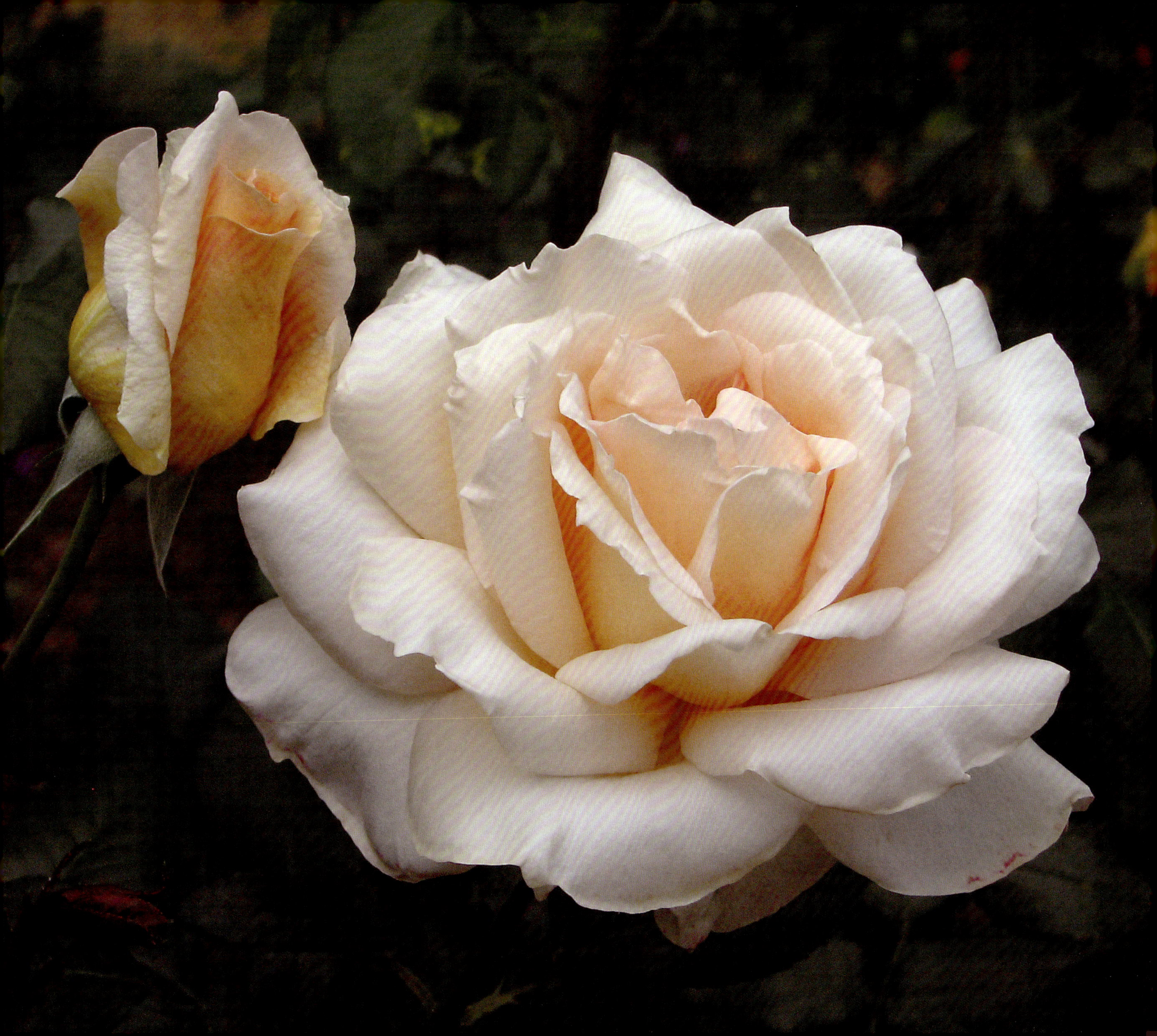

In mid-spring to early summer the roses along the pergola unfold into a rich tapestry of glorious colour, with climbing roses wreathing the pillars and crossbeams with a myriad blooms.

PART 1

THE PERGOLA

A pergola, a shady walkway covered by a canopy of plants, was first introduced to Italian gardens many generations ago. Columns, swathed in decorative climbing plants with crossbeams over which they can grow to provide shade, are a fine addition to any large garden. Well-constructed benches at the ends of the walk or one in the middle will be an invitation to all to relax and enjoy the scene. Include some sweetly scented climbers with those chosen and you will have a beguiling place from which to watch your garden grow.

The pergola at Old Nectar developed along the graceful curve made by the old main road as it passed the house. This had been closed and a new main road nearer the river had been constructed five years before we acquired the property. The well-made surface of the old gravel road therefore became the broad path of the pergola. The problem that confronted me before we started making the pillars was to know how far apart to site them and how high they should be. I spent a great deal of time sketching outlines of the idea and eventually came to a decision that proved to be the correct one, for the proportions are pleasing and harmonious.

Dante's helper during the months spent making the pillars was a young policeman from southern Italy who loved opera and was constantly singing arias from Verdi as he shaped the bricks to make the base of each of the 42 pillars more ornamental. Finally a bench was made in the middle of the pergola where the main path from the house meets it.

The choice of plants to decorate the pillars took several months. Climbing roses there had to be, but as they flower mainly in spring, there should also be climbers to bring colour during the other seasons of the year. We now have plants from many countries weaving their way up the pillars and across the wooden beams to give shade during our very hot summers. There are jasmines of different kinds, honeysuckle and wisteria to provide fragrance, and various bignonias, clematis, combretum, golden shower, aristolochia, sky flower, guinea gold vine and yellow trumpet climber to introduce leaf interest and colourful flowers.

But it is not only the climbers that bring beauty to the pergola. The trees and shrubs planted alongside – camellias, cherries, crabapples, magnolias, maples and ornamental peach – all contribute to the vibrant and delightful scenes that appear as one walks its length.

ABOVE: *This bush rose named South Africa, planted five years ago, is a lovely addition.*

TOP: *A delightful climbing rose envelops the pillar in the pergola where it grows, producing lovely single flowers of deep pink.*

LEFT: *Wisteria is worth growing for its scent alone. Here it is the first of the climbers to produce flowers very early in spring. The lovely flowers hang down elegantly from the drooping stems and make the area where they grow look entrancing, but for too short a time, as the flowering is generally over in four weeks. The scent of the flowers attracts bumble bees that whirl around all day long collecting nectar. They appear only when the scent of the wisteria is strong and disappear as soon as the flowers fade. Where do they go for the other 48 weeks of the year? The trimmed golden privet adds colour to the scene through the year.*

ABOVE: *Carolina jasmine.* This evergreen plant with willowy stems may attain a height and spread of 4 m. It has ovate, shining, light-green leaves up to 10 cm long which are ornamental throughout the year. In late winter and early spring it carries cascades of lightly fragrant, golden, funnel-shaped flowers up to 3 cm long.

ABOVE RIGHT: *Mexican blood trumpet vine* is a handsome evergreen and a strong grower which climbs by means of tendrils to 9 m or more, if it is not trimmed back. From spring to autumn it bears clusters of magnificent, large, trumpet-shaped flowers of a luminous coral-red, flushed with yellow in the throat. The plant needs a strong support to keep it erect. It can be trained along a fence to form a hedge, over a large pergola or patio for shade or shelter, against the walls of the house, or up into a tree.

RIGHT: We found an attractive fanlight-shaped piece in a metal junkyard and used it to make the back of the bench shown in the picture opposite.

ABOVE: *Golden shower is one of the very few climbing plants that bear flowers in autumn and winter. The bright-green glossy leaves are a fine foil for its brilliant orange flowers. Train it over an arbour, pergola or trellis to shade a patio. A mature plant should be trimmed back in spring to keep it from taking over too much of the garden. Here it partly frames the mountain opposite.*

LEFT: *Along the sides of the pergola, between the pillars, bush roses and irises add colour for eight months of the year. The background shrub is a variegated abutilon.*

OPPOSITE *Gold Bunny is the name of this lovely yellow climbing rose which bears a mass of flowers in mid-to-late spring.*

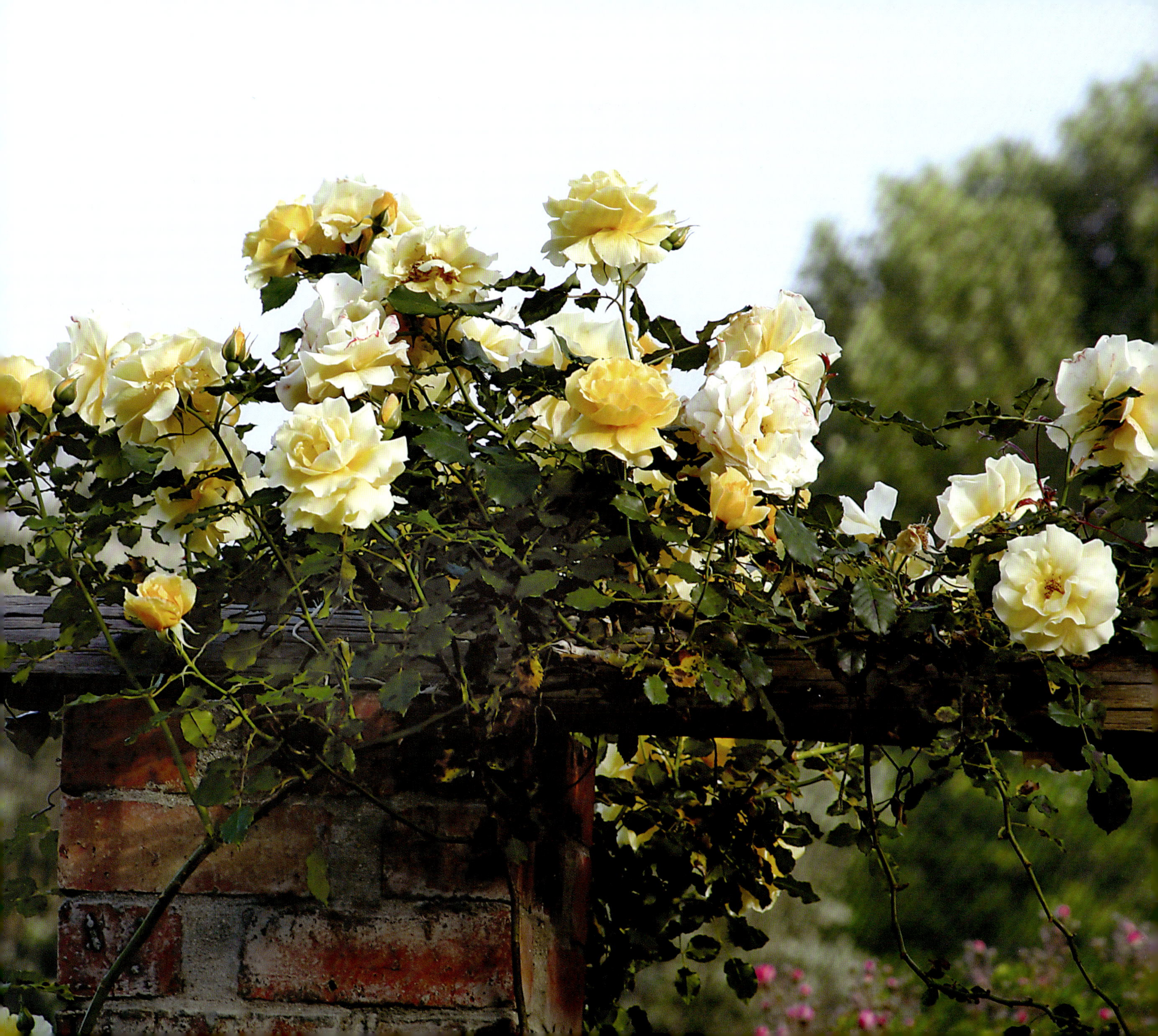

ABOVE: *This rose, which bears a profusion of flowers of a delightful shade of rose-pink, is Little Pink Hedge. It has the additional attribute of having pretty glossy foliage.*

OPPOSITE: *By midsummer most of the pillars are swathed in their mantle of leaves. Here the steep bank on the edge of the pergola is covered with plants. The roses are Iceberg, Fiery Sensation and Pinkie, surrounding a bronze berberis.*

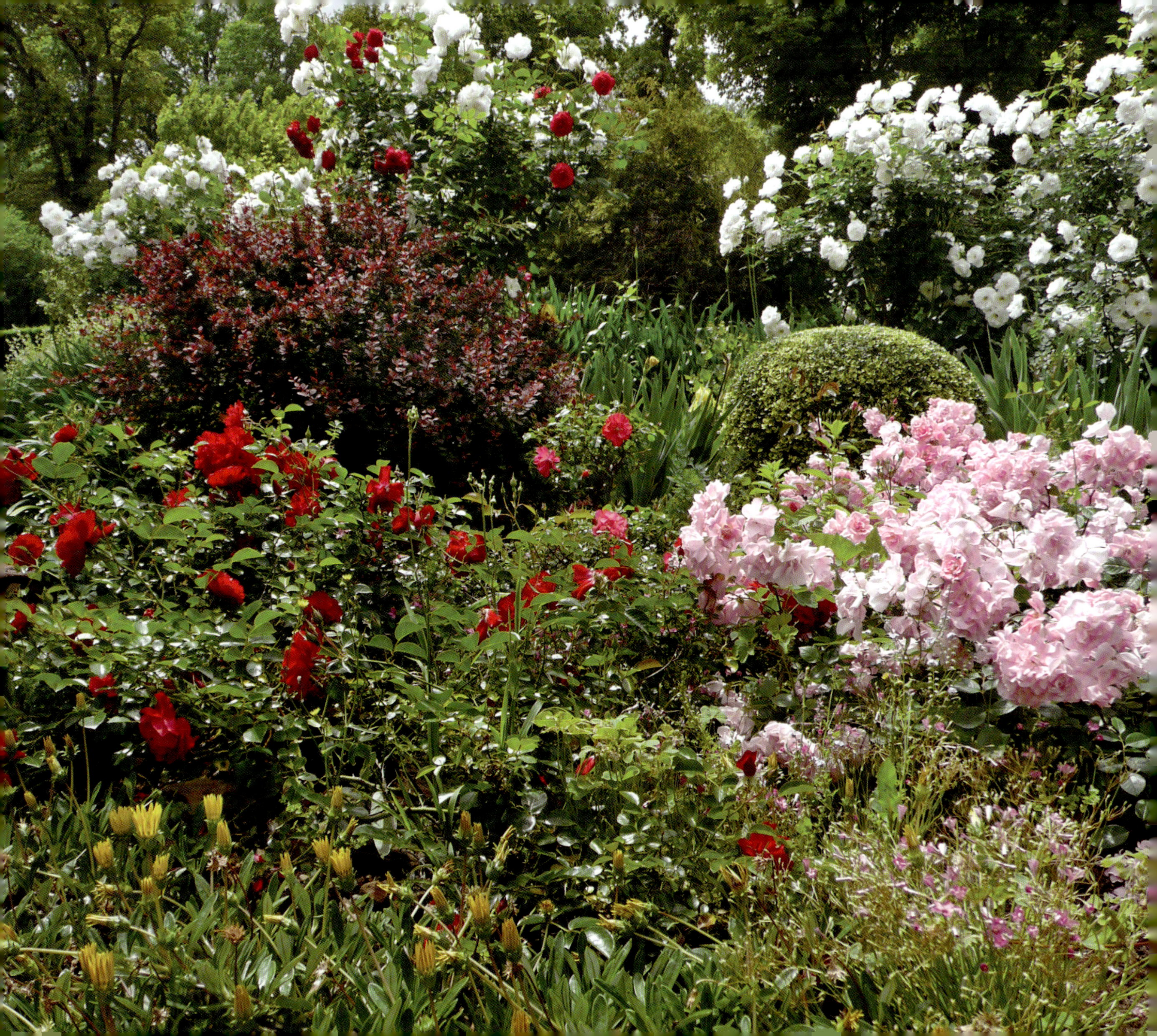

This ornamental peach is one of the first of the flowering fruits to highlight the garden early in spring. It is preceded by the ornamental plum and is followed by the crabapple. It makes a wonderful show for several weeks and is a fine tree for the small-to-medium garden as it does not spread too far and wide.

Indeed a glory to behold – as one walks along the pergola one comes across this wonderful combination of two lovely plants in full flower – a Japanese cherry, Kanzan, and a snowball.

Hybrid clematis produce their flowers of ethereal loveliness in spring to early summer. There are numerous named cultivars some of which are available at a few nurseries. They do not grow and flower as well here as they do in Europe but they are well worth planting. This close-up shows how the central boss of stamens adds beauty to the flowers.

ABOVE: *The texture of the flowers of this clematis reminds one of old brocade.*

TOP: Clematis montana *is one of many different types of clematis. Its dainty flowers measuring about 10 cm across are white, pale pink or deep rose and adorn the plant like a cloud of butterflies.*

RIGHT: *And this one of royal purple appears to float in the air.*

ABOVE: *Here a clematis has made its way up into the branches of a crabapple with flowers of pink and white.*

OPPOSITE: *Where the main path from the house joins the pergola, it passes beneath an exceptionally beautiful old cornelian-coloured camellia which shades the path. The camellia flowers all winter long. We leave the fallen flowers to decorate the path for several days and then add them to the compost.*

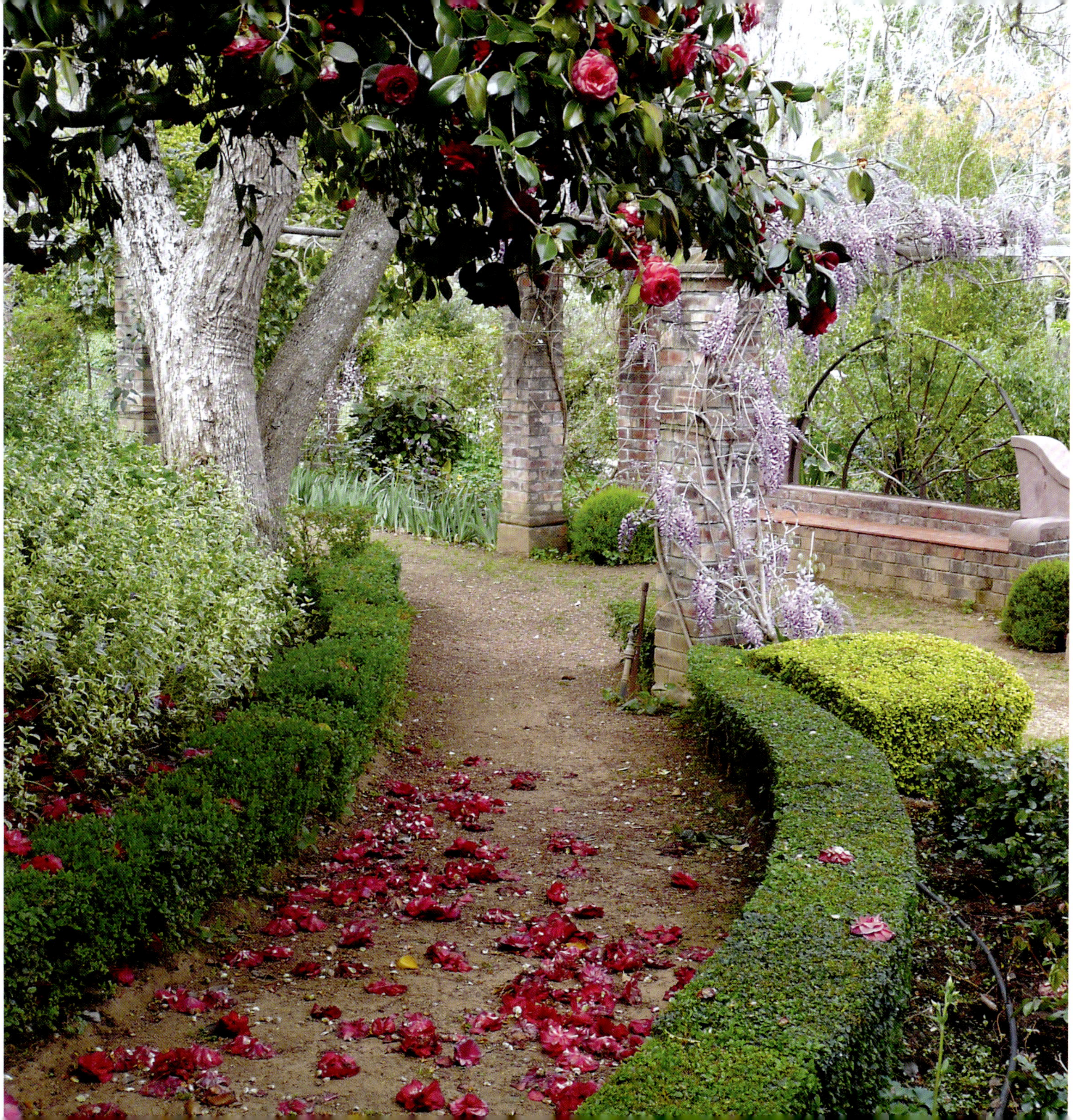

ABOVE: *The bush rose, Gold Bunny, flowers on and off for most of the warm months of the year.*

ABOVE LEFT: *At the western end of the pergola one comes across this pleasing combination of red and white climbing roses around the pillars.*

LEFT: *Rose varieties with a shrub-like form and clusters of flowers are a good contrast to those of upright growth*

OPPOSITE: *Star jasmine is an attractive evergreen twining plant which makes a verdant curtain over a wall or bank, or a pergola or arbour to provide shade beneath. It can also be grown as a ground cover in a large garden. Its ovate, shining leaves are about 5 cm in length, and show up to perfection the delicate white flowers which appear in spring and summer in loose clusters. Their enchanting fragrance and delicate beauty add to its charm.*

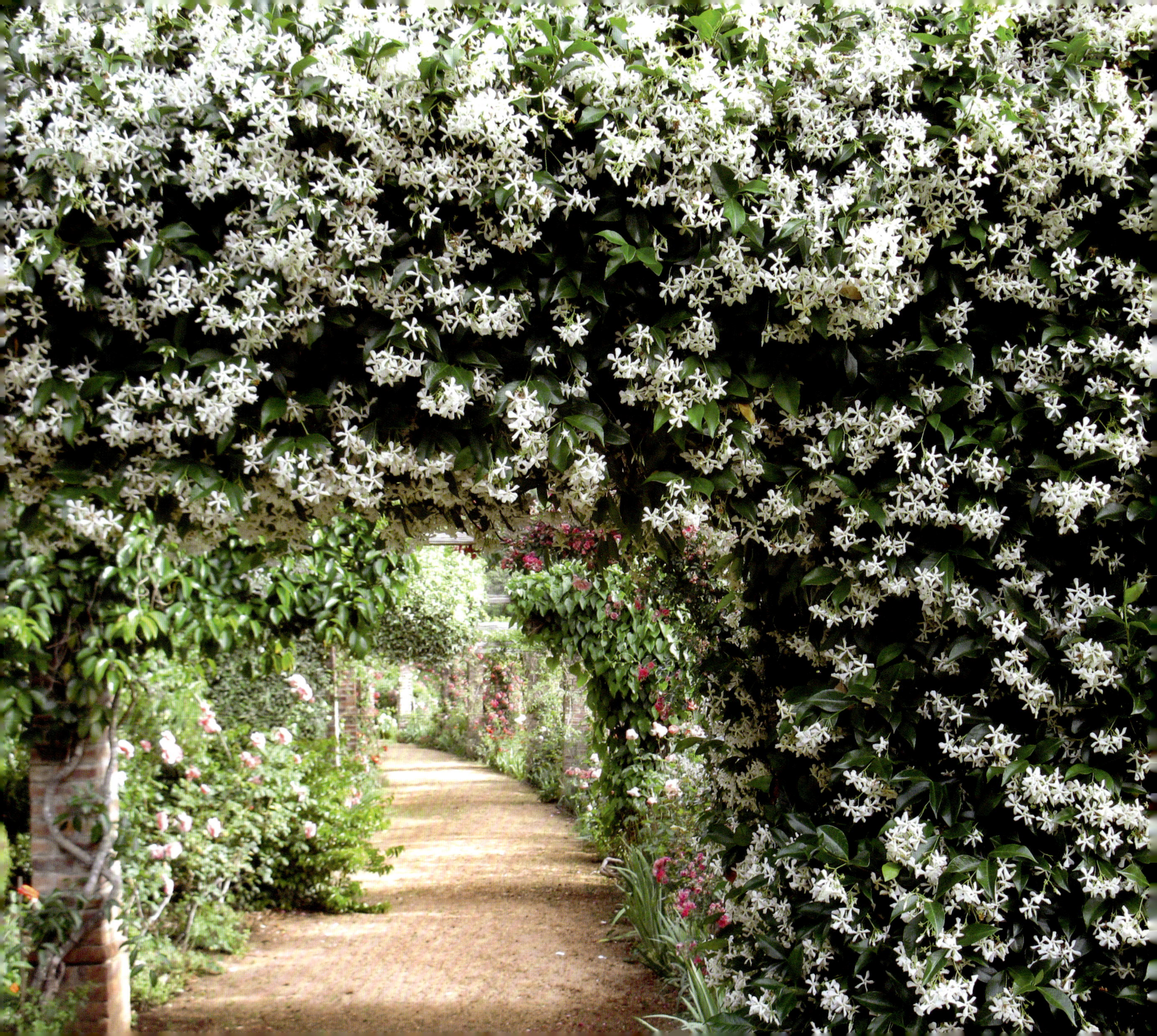

An enchanting corner of the woodland garden where a rough bench invites one to sit beneath the birches and enjoy the scene. A Japanese maple flaunts its beauty near an exquisite azalea.

PART 1

THE WOODLAND GARDEN

As one reaches the north-western end of the pergola, one comes upon a narrow curving brick path turning right – an invitation to leave the rather grand, wide walkway of the pergola and explore where it leads. Here one enters the woodland garden, a different scene. A diversity of plants – trees, shrubs, climbers and smaller ones – combine to create a woodland through which the narrow path meanders with several curves, and around each bend a new vista appears.

The scenes change all the time as the seasons come and go, but whatever the season, this garden engenders feelings of peace and harmony. Here one lingers to enjoy the sights and sounds of nature – the frolicking squirrels, the singing birds and the chirping insects.

In early spring the new leaves of Japanese maples beckon and, moving along, one marvels at the beauty of the last flowers of a camellia and the new ones of the ornamental peach. The camellias are shaded by the still-bare branches of a crabapple, and nearby a Japanese cherry with its silky ash-colour bark attracts the eye. At various points along the curving path azaleas make vivid splashes of colour in the dappled shade and, when they start to fade, the green globes of the flowers of the snowball bush festoon the plant like Christmas decorations. By mid-spring the crabapples and the cherries produce their lovely blossoms, as abundant as the stars in the sky, an enchanting scene. The roses and irises along the way see this as a challenge and put on a spectacular show as well.

When summer comes the trees and shrubs are in full leaf and one is grateful for the dense canopy of their shade. Gone are the vibrant colours of spring, replaced now by the different shades of green and by the white and blue of agapanthus and hydrangeas. Hugging the sides of the paths are smaller flowers such as impatiens and begonia and here and there is a lily.

In autumn, when the leaves of trees and shrubs begin to colour, there are swathes of the snow-white Japanese anemone to delight the eye. They make a fine contrast to the yellowing leaves.

During the first weeks of winter, the woodland garden is a glorious scene with a canopy and carpets of leaves coloured from bright yellow to amber, through shades of gold and rose to a rich crimson hue. The golden-yellow ones are those of the ginkgo, which is a magnificent sight for three to four weeks before all its leaves fall. The others are those of the cherries and maples, the snowball and the spice bush. Camellias are at their best during winter and produce their lovely flowers – white, palest pink, rose and crimson – through the coldest months. Near ground level the unique flowers of hellebores show up well against their ornate leaves and, when all the leaves have fallen, the four tree magnolias in this area put on their wonderful winter show – ash-grey branches bearing a myriad sculptured flowers coloured soft mauve with a flush of pink; and, at their feet, the perky snowflakes, not to be outdone, send up their nodding little snow-white flowers.

62

ABOVE: *The fan-shaped golden leaves of the ginkgo tree are a glorious sight for the first month of winter. They are so bright and uniform in colour that they command attention from many parts of the garden.*

RIGHT: *The ornamental peach trees on the left and in the distance are a joyous sight early in spring as one walks along this stone path in the woodland garden. The leaves of agapanthus form a handsome border to the path.*

OPPOSITE PAGE

FAR LEFT: *Bearded irises grow in many parts of the garden and flower even when neglected. These canary-yellow hybrids beckon one to follow the brick path into the woodland garden where it leaves the pergola.*

ABOVE: *And here one meets a snow-white azalea – the old favourite grown a century ago – reliable and with the additional merit of having vanilla-scented flow*

BELOW: *There are now thousands of cultivars of azaleas available. This is a happy mixture of two different kinds and contrasting colours.*

ABOVE: *Hellebores are delightful plants to grow in areas with light shade. Their leaves make a permanent ground cover and the flowers on stems 45 cm tall appear from late autumn until mid-spring.*

LEFT: *Here the stone path leads past banks of azaleas of different shades. They form a wonderful screen between the woodland garden and the pergola.*

ABOVE: *Crabapples do best where winters are cold. They are suitable for small-to-medium gardens as they can be pruned to prevent them from growing too high and wide. The myriad of small blossoms dance in every breeze that blows.*

RIGHT: *The fragile petals of a cherry fall like confetti to make a bridal walk.*

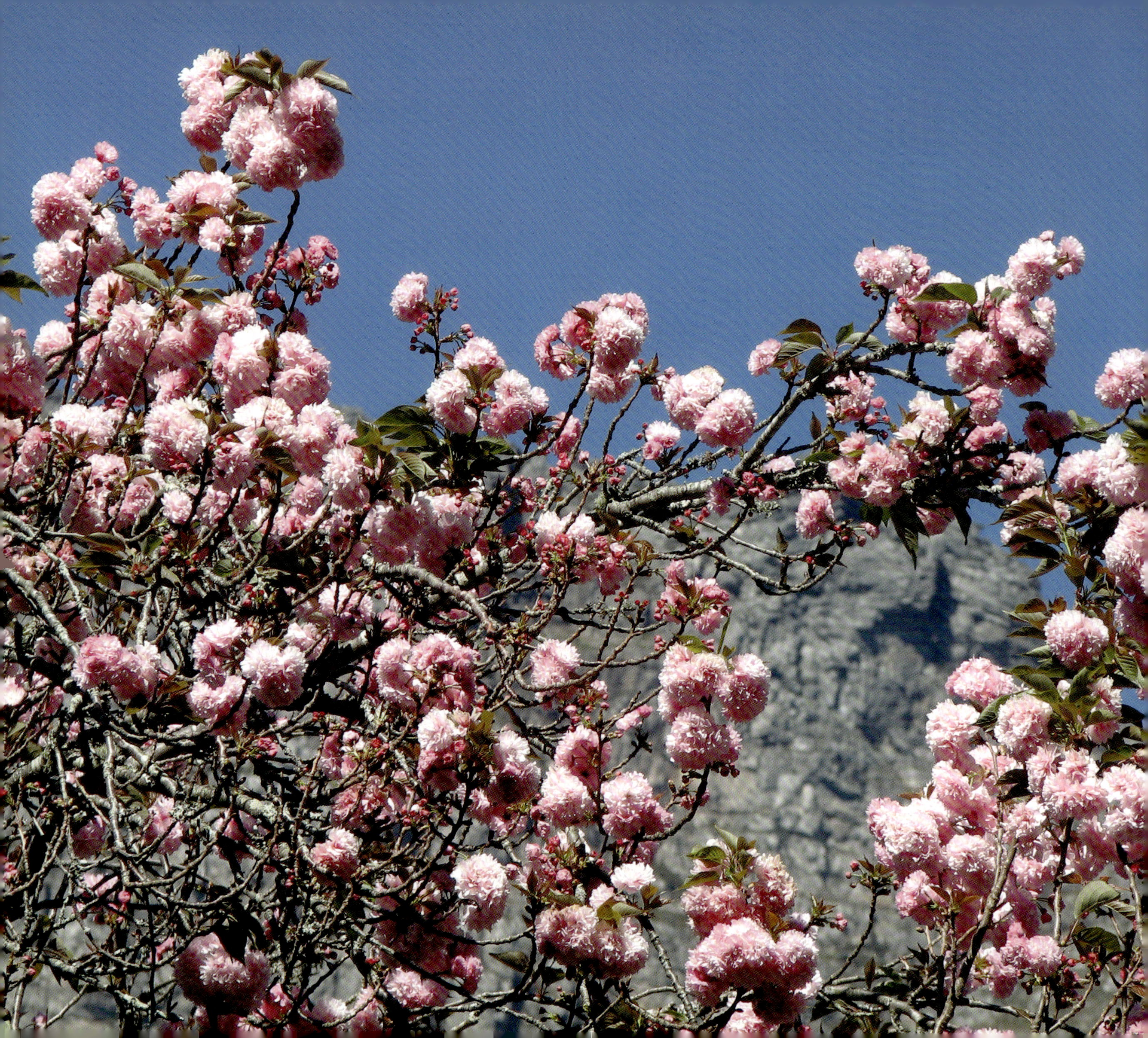

ABOVE: *The spice bush is worth growing for its leaves, which have a strong scent and taste of spice when picked and chewed. In autumn the handsome leaves turn gold.*

ABOVE RIGHT: *We planted four birches only about a metre apart, as they would grow in their natural environment, to form a strong central feature to the woodland garden. The bench is the meeting point between the brick path and the stone one. The shape of the boulder is repeated in the small trimmed privet.*

RIGHT: *Pride of India is the only small tree I know that has an abundance of flowers in summer. Here its brightly coloured flowers enhance the one end of the pergola and the entrance to the woodland garden in the unrelenting heat of February.*

OPPOSITE: *The Japanese cherry is one of the most ornamental of all trees, for not only does it have an abundance of blossom in spring but the leaves assume wonderful colours in late autumn and winter.*

ABOVE: *The pieris is decorative in early spring when new ruby-red leaves emerge, and even more attractive later when it flowers.*

TOP: *As the leaves fall from the ginkgo tree they turn from bright yellow to mustard on the steps and path.*

LEFT: *Campsis is a handsome summer-flowering climber that carries large clusters of flowers that glow in colour against its pretty leaves.*

ABOVE: *This lovely camellia flower is one of the thousands of blooms that appear on the plants during winter.*

ABOVE RIGHT: *When summer comes hydrangeas produce their showy flowers, which last for three to four months, changing colour as they fade.*

RIGHT: *The snow-white flowers of Japanese anemones brighten the area where they grow for weeks in autumn. They are produced on long, graceful stems 60 cm high or more and have decorative vine-shaped leaves which hide the ground for much of the year.*

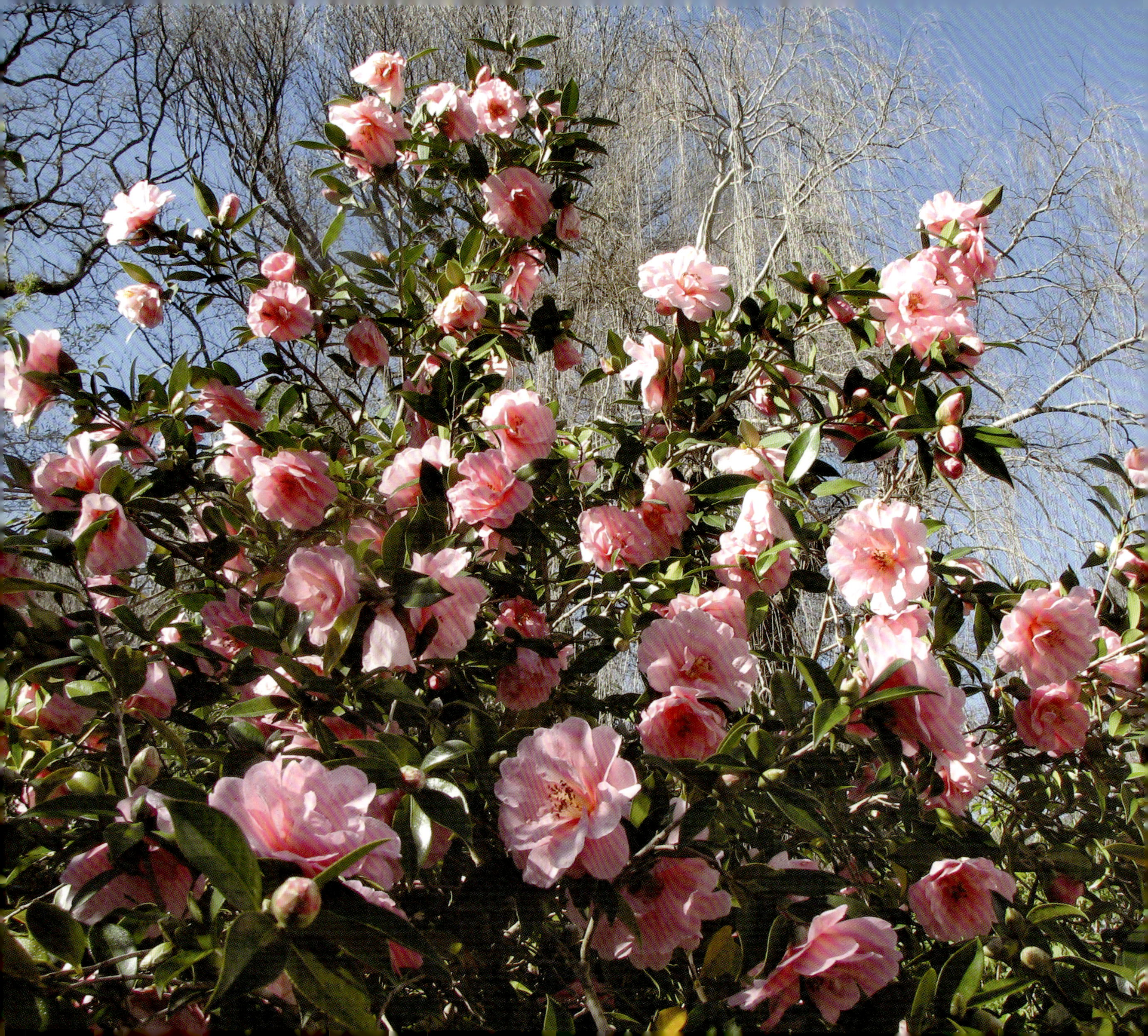

PART 1

THE BENCH GARDEN

Turn left when leaving the woodland garden, move up a few steps decorated by two small white urns, and you face, on the left, garden number five, generally known as the bench garden. It is one of my favourite areas (except for the bench). A wide grass path bordered by very low hedges leads to the bench that is to me an eyesore, but I cannot change it. My husband made it despite my protestations. And thereby hangs a tale.

He grew up in an era when most people had very low incomes and nothing was wasted. When the bed sheets began to wear in the middle, they were cut in half and the edges sewn together. When the collars of shirts became frayed, they were "turned" so that the frayed side was beneath. During the Boer War, when he was eight years old, his mother, a young Englishwoman, insisted on leaving Stellenbosch and going to live amongst those whom she considered the victims of British injustice and to work with them in Pretoria. Three years later his father, a descendant of the first Van der Spuy who left Holland in the late 17th century, died, and within another year his mother died of pneumonia. There were no relatives in the Transvaal, so the three children, of whom my husband, aged 12, was the youngest, had to fend for themselves from then on. His first job was as a 'messenger boy' running errands for a shop. This was followed by a better-paid one as a clerk in a bank in Pretoria. By this time he had started evening classes and in due course passed matric. At 18 he started work at the Observatory in Johannesburg and, two years later, became a pupil pilot in the embryonic South African Flying School at Kimberley. At 21 he qualified as a pilot in the Royal Flying Corps, which in 1918 became the Royal Air Force, and was flying in France in 1914 as part of the British forces fighting the Germans. He was one of the first South Africans to qualify as a military pilot. At 55 he retired as a Major-General.

There is a lesson here for all of us – aim for the stars and ensure that you get there! It was only natural that his approach towards life was to 'make use of everything'.

When, in 1942, soon after my arrival at Old Nectar, we were putting in two bathrooms, there were no tiles available, as these had always been imported, and by then all shipping between England and the Cape carried only war materials. My husband was friendly with the Cullinan family of Pretoria, one of whose ancestors had owned the mine which produced the famous diamond of that name. They had a large brickyard near Pretoria. Walking around the brickyard with the owner, whose bricks had now been requisitioned by the army to build accommodation for army recruits, he happened to see a mass of bathroom tiles lying on the dusty ground. Just what we need, he thought, and made arrangements to rail them all to Stellenbosch. The tiles had

OPPOSITE: *With many different camellias being offered by nurseries, it is not easy to select one for the garden as there are no descriptive catalogues and the nurserymen have no pictures of the flowers. It is wise, therefore, to make a choice in winter when they are in flower. The exceptionally lovely one pictured here is called Donation. I do not know the names of the others in the garden as, when I bought them, they had no labels.*

The broad lawn path, edged by low hedges backed by azaleas, is a colourful scene in spring and very beautiful in winter too, when the maples turn russet, the tall ginkgo in the adjoining woodland garden becomes daffodil-yellow, and the magnolias and the camellias are in full flower.

been made by the grandfather of the then owners during the 1914–18 war, and had lain there ever since, for 24 years.

They were mostly green, much thicker than the usual bathroom tiles, highly glazed and with old-fashioned patterns embellishing their surfaces. Unfortunately there were several different patterns and I had to lay them out on the stoep and arrange and rearrange them in order to find the right numbers of tiles for any one room – the kitchen, the pantry, the lobby, the bathrooms. The last but 50 of them were used on the swimming pool.

After my husband had retired he found a box containing the few remaining tiles in the old cellar, now a storage place for tools and fertilisers, and decided that they had to be used to make a bench, despite my objections – and, there it is, decorated with tiles of green, brown, deep blue and mustard yellow. I cannot destroy it now that he is no longer here; it wouldn't be fair. And last year I was shown an English book dealing with gardening in which appeared an illustration of this very bench.

Two years ago as I was telling this story to a Johannesburg visitor, she said, 'But Una, you've got a fortune there. Those tiles are now selling as antiques in Johannesburg at R250 per tile.' That may well be, but his bench will remain to remind me: 'Use everything; waste nothing.'

The bench garden is more formal than any other part of the garden and therefore attractive throughout the year because of its definite lines. For this reason, I always recommend that those who have neither the time nor the inclination to garden, should make a formal garden. It requires only regular mowing of the lawn and cutting of the hedges to keep it pleasing, whereas, if not given regular attention, an informal garden that is furnished with a larger variety of plants can soon become a wilderness if the plants are allowed to grow into one another.

This small area of lawn is cut by a manual mower, as are the other four small lawns at the side and behind the house. I often wonder why the owners of small gardens buy a power mower. Using a manual one, one can cut the lawn in the garden of average size in about 20 minutes, provided it is done regularly. Power and electric mowers are heavier to handle and to my mind generally more bother.

The bench garden is attractive all the year round, and it is ravishing in September when the azaleas behind the low hedges come into flower and in winter when the camellias and the magnolias bear their lovely flowers.

From this garden we move up six steps and are level with the base of the house.

ABOVE RIGHT: *The approach to the bench garden from the house is via the steps down to the second lawn terrace in front of the house. As one cannot see it from the house, it is a concealed and pleasant surprise.*

RIGHT: *… and the path to the bench garden from the pergola has on one side a holly and on the other the largest camellia in the garden with the rose Pinkie adding colour for much of the year. Then up seven steps to reach the second terrace and the bench garden on the same level.*

ABOVE: *This is one of the many beautiful azaleas growing here.*

ABOVE LEFT: *A view from the bench garden towards the pergola, where the height of the azaleas forms a lovely screen between the two areas.*

LEFT: *This delightful azalea shines out from the shade cast by the silver birches.*

OPPOSITE PAGE

LEFT: *Growing behind the azaleas are seven camellias with flowers of different colours, from white through palest pink to rose and crimson. All our camellias are now large shrubs or small trees three to four metres tall. These are two of them.*

RIGHT: *The four birches in the woodland garden, hidden from view, make a wonderful backdrop to the bench garden throughout the year. The scene is very beautiful in winter when their silver boles and branches are etched against the cobalt sky.*

75

Agapanthus decorate the steep bank above the azaleas …

… and these hydrangeas nestle next to the bench.

On either side of the broad lawn path are winter-flowering magnolias (M. soulangeana) – a small spreading tree with ash-grey branches that carry hundreds of handsome pinky-mauve flowers for two months in winter. They make a splendid show as most of the surrounding trees are then bare of leaves.

This is the view that greets one from the dining room in spring. All the senses are involved. The eyes are delighted; there is the scent of the brunfelsia to breathe in; the murmur of the water and the song of the birds are here plainly heard; and one is tempted to stroke the smooth leaves of the cannas or to pick a twig of the lavender; or taste the lemon balm.

PART 1

THE BACK GARDEN

The back garden is glorious in spring, peaceful and pleasing in summer and autumn, but rather dreary for two months in winter.

It is the most lived-in part of the garden as it is on a level with the house, with doors leading on to it from the dining room and the kitchen. Here, during late spring, summer and early autumn, we have breakfast and often also dinner on a summer evening. It is too hot in the middle of the day in summer and too wet in winter. The whole area is the size of the average town garden; the lawn measures only 44 square metres.

After finishing the terracing for lawns in the front of the house, I tackled this area, first because it was so unsightly, and, secondly, because I needed somewhere on the same level as the house to serve al fresco meals. It had been a dumping ground for generations. Pieces of broken crockery, bits of harness and other old farming equipment emerged as we dug over the ground.

Facing the house and only 31 metres away was an old slave cottage. There was no wall or screen of plants between the house and the cottage. It was easy to plan and plant a barrier of tall evergreen shrubs and climbers to make the area private and cosy. I chose cestrum, brunfelsia, moonflower, hibiscus and cotoneaster, the climber petrea and the climbing rose Crepuscule to serve this purpose.

From this small area we had a good view of the famous Twin Peaks of the mountain range, and I decided to emphasise the mountain view and so make it the focal point of this garden. Careful planning was necessary. I hit upon the idea of framing the Peaks with two noble trees and having a waterfall in the foreground to draw the eye to them. This entailed having to redirect the flow of a small mountain stream that started on my neighbour's farm on the slope above and flowed on the far side of our property down to the river.

As the waterfall was to be three metres high, we needed a number of large rocks, so, nothing daunted, we used fencing posts to lever out rocks from the ground on the far side of the property and eventually got them into place to form the waterfall. Then, there had to be a pool at the base of the waterfall. Having already made a large swimming pool, we found making a small lily pool was no problem.

Thereafter came the planting around the pool. Unfortunately I decided to plant a willow, and what a bother this has been ever since. It sends its major roots far and wide and produces also masses of small roots that greedily absorb whatever water we apply to other plants in the area. Every year I decide to have the willow removed, but my resolve weakens when I realise that this would spoil the background.

I planted two liquidambars to frame the Twin Peaks. They give me much pleasure all the year through and particularly in autumn when their leaves turn brilliant colours. Liquidambar is one of the finest of the American trees, but suitable only for large gardens.

The sound of the falling water and the sunlight glistening on it add animation to the scene, and I often think that every garden of moderate size could create a similar scene using smaller trees in the background. The water would, of course, have to be circulated by means of a pump.

In our hot climate a water feature is, to my mind, an essential to add a feeling of life and coolness to the garden. It could be as small as a birdbath or a small fountain, but preferably a small pool that reflects the plants around it.

The stream that comes over the waterfall is a raging torrent during the rainy season and we have to divert the water into a storm-water drain, and, in the dry period of the year, we sometimes have to circulate the water by means of a pump as the stream tends to dry up.

The most beautiful of the plants in this garden is the Japanese maple. I give its full botanical name as there are so many different maples. It is *Acer palmatum dissectum atropureum*. All maples fall under the botanical name of *Acer*. *Palmatum* indicates that the leaves are like the palm of a hand. *Dissectum* describes the very finely cut leaves and *atropureum* means the leaves are of a purple (really bronze) colour. This is an exceptionally attractive shrub for gardens large and small, planted in the ground or in a large pot.

I bought this precious plant within two years of my arrival at Old Nectar, when I knew very little and, unfortunately, Mr Brunning's book did not mention it. The result: I planted it in the wrong place – in the hottest part of the garden where it would also get reflected light from a white wall. These maples require filtered shade and, even in the cooler climate of Europe, they are grown under trees. The main reason why I chose this particular position was that this small plant cost the exorbitant sum of £5 – in today's money R200 – and I therefore decided it should be where I could easily watch its progress day by day. Each spring I eagerly look forward to the emergence of its so enchanting tiny, tiny, new bronze leaves. One can almost see them growing larger during the day. Unfortunately the heat of February scorches them.

Much of the colour in this area is provided by the foliage of the various shrubs and ground covers. The shrubs are golden abelia and golden privet, dusty miller and the gazania with silver leaves that grows flat against the ground. There are two groups of cannas; one has leaves

LEFT: *This rich mixture of colour makes a spectacular show in spring: the vivid colours of the petrea and Japanese maple with the gold of a rambler rose behind.*

of a rich burgundy colour and the other has gold-striped leaves. The two small trees immediately above the waterfall with pretty, golden leaves are robinia, a hybrid of *Robinia pseudacacia*.

Over the small building nearby that was the dairy when I arrived here, and subsequently became my husband's office and is now a kennel, I planted yellow and white climbing roses and a Virginia creeper to hide its unsightliness. In my opinion, Virginia creeper is the ideal climber to camouflage a large wall or fence as it has little sucker-like discs that cling tightly to the wall and one does not have to fasten it to the surface. Its leaves are glossy and it makes a splendid show in autumn when they become brilliantly coloured, burnished copper to crimson.

On the eastern side of this area is a rhododendron seven metres tall which bears handsome clusters of rich ruby-red flowers in spring. It came from Nepal.

About 25 years ago I joined a group to visit and do a hike in Nepal. The objective was to walk to where rhododendrons grow in their natural habitat in the foothills of the Himalayas. I'm not a mountain walker, nor was my sister, who also joined the expedition. The time allocated for the walk part of the tour was four days. The alternative offered to those who did not wish to walk was to visit a jungle and ride on an elephant to look for tigers!

My sister, then aged 75, who had never walked more than a kilometre in her life and never on a mountain, opted for the ride. Our first four days in Kathmandu were spent visiting the historic sites and temples in the vicinity. During this time we became acquainted with the other 24 members of the group. They were mostly grey-haired and somewhat overweight and I began to doubt that they would manage a four-day mountain walk. I had also begun to believe that my sister might fall off the elephant and perhaps become a tasty meal for the tiger, so I persuaded her to change her arrangements and join the walk. Of course

RIGHT: *Looking towards the old dairy with its bower of climbing roses, one sees in the foreground, growing in the stone wall, a ground cover interplanted with pelargoniums to hang over the wall, with shrubby, low-growing roses in the foreground.*

she had no suitable shoes and had to buy a pair. The shoes she chose were flimsy canvas with a strap, so back she had to go to change them for something more substantial as, by this time, I had discovered that most of those doing the walk had brought along proper mountain-climbing boots.

On our fifth day in Nepal we left our hotel at dawn and were joined by 15 sherpas to fetch, carry, put up tents and generally ensure our well-being. It seemed a large number for only 20 hikers, but in the end we really needed them all because near disaster struck within the first three hours when two members of the party began to feel ill. Soon after we started out, leeches began to attach themselves to us, nasty things that seemed to drop from space and immediately suck fast on to a limb. Fortunately the sherpas were quick to notice this and took immediate action. The nearest of the sherpas, all of whom smoked, would use the tip of his cigarette to get them to fall off one's arms and legs.

The paths were narrow and stony and there were innumerable rivers to cross. Most of them were shallow but, as they were very broad and had beds of round stones, many of the walkers fell down into the water at least once during the crossing of each river. I found this hilarious: large bodies recumbent in the water being helped to their feet by the little sherpas. It really was an amusing sight. As it was a hot day, nobody was going to suffer from a little wetting. Eventually the sherpas decided that they should carry people over the rivers and thus we progressed, step by difficult step, up and down hill after hill, gaining altitude all the time. It was not really mountain-climbing but steep hill-walking. By lunch-time the leader of the group had taken ill and his deputy was keeping to the rear of the very spread-out party in order to help and reassure those at the back. To my astonishment now heading the group was my sister and she continued to be in front until half an hour before we reached our camp at dusk, when in a cloudburst of rain a large, youngish male member of the party came to the front. When I got to the camp as number three, I asked my sister how she had managed to walk so fast all the way. She replied: 'When I saw all those people in their climbing boots I thought that I might be left behind so, mind over matter, I kept to the front.' She was a great believer in the positive force of 'mind over matter' and lived to the age of 96, with no rheumatism or any of the afflictions of old age, except poor eyesight.

It pelted with rain all the time the sherpas were putting up our small two-man tents. In the meanwhile, by the light of lanterns the cooks had prepared a large meal and, although we went to bed wet, we certainly were not hungry.

The morning dawned bright but mist veiled all views at first. When it suddenly evaporated we found ourselves part of an awesome Himalayan landscape. We were in the midst of an endless vista of majestic, towering, snow-clad peaks – a most impressive and glorious scene sharply etched on one's memory for all time. Those who were not feeling fit then started their descent whilst the rest of the group continued higher and found ourselves in a forest of rhododendrons – trees up to ten metres. As it was autumn none was in flower. It was from these trees that I got the plant that now enhances my back garden.

This area near the kitchen is home also to six camellias, a luculia, two of the oldest of the climbing roses planted 60 years ago, a holly with variegated leaves, and ground covers of hellebore for winter colour, bluebells for spring and impatiens for summer.

OPPOSITE: *This dearly loved maple is most co-operative for, in my ignorance, I planted it in the sunniest and warmest place on the property 62 years ago. Its requirements are a cool shady position. Nevertheless, it produces its ethereal, lace-like leaves of ruby-red with the first breath of spring as though this was the ideal ambience. How generous, kind and forgiving!*

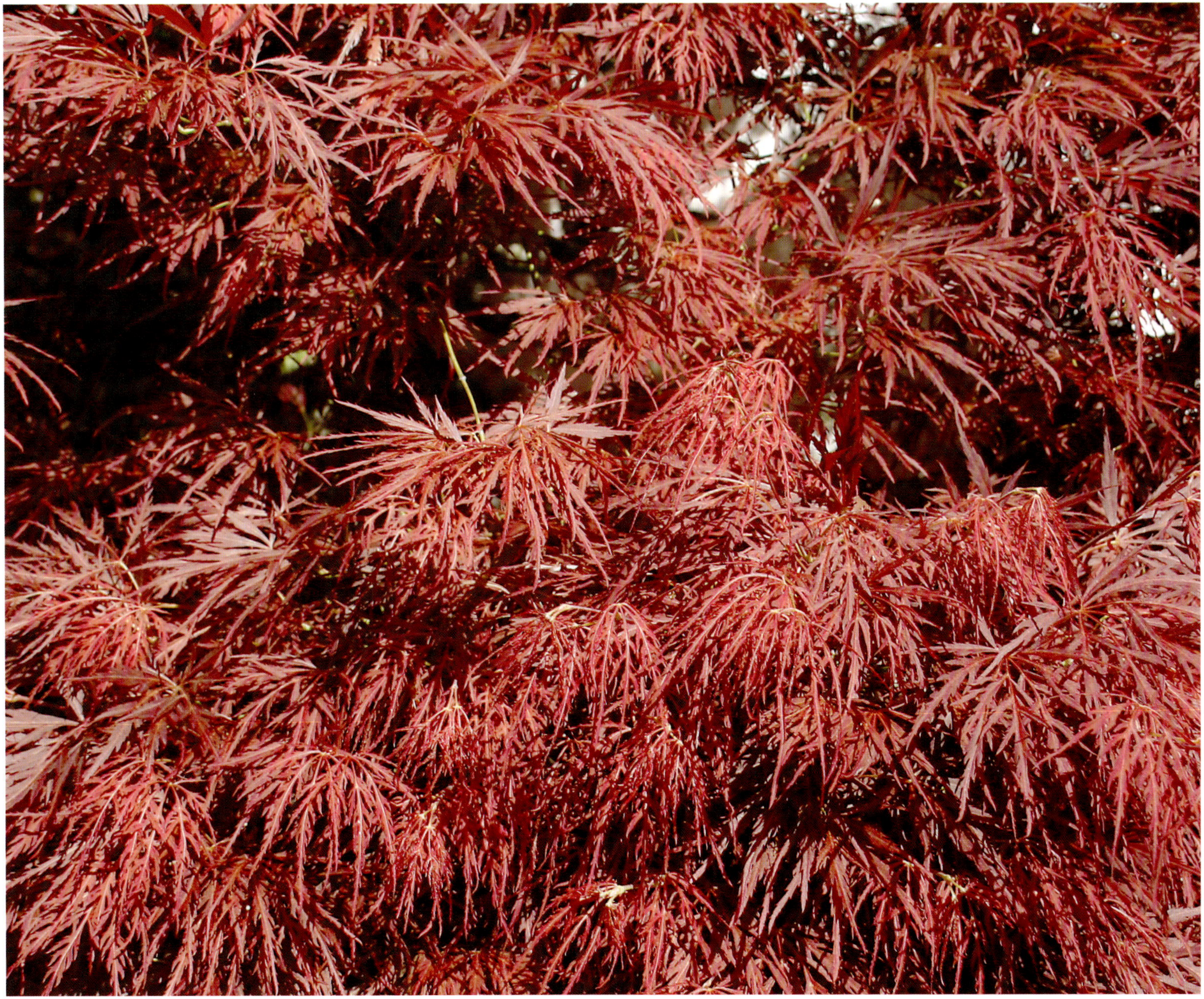

The ugly old dairy has done a Cinderella act and emerged beautifully gowned – in a rich mantle of Virginia creeper with climbing roses for adornment. The golden robinia in the background is a splendid tree for small gardens and the variegated abutilon in front of it can be relied on to thrive even if the watering system fails, as it sometimes does. Cannas of burgundy and gold provide colour on both sides of the waterfall for most months of the year.

The climbing rose Crepuscule is a lovely screen between the garden and the old slave cottage just beyond. Dusty miller, berberis, golden privet, golden abelia and bronze cannas provide colour throughout the year.

ABOVE: *Moses-in-the-bulrushes seems a cumbersome name for this small waterside plant that hugs the bank around the pool.*

LEFT: *These gold-striped canna leaves are ornamental through most of the year. The flowers are removed because we feel they spoil the scene.*

This rhododendron from Nepal, now 25 years old, makes a striking background on the eastern side of this small garden.

ABOVE: *A yellow banksia rose against the wall of the old dairy starts flowering in late winter and makes a canopy of gold all through spring. It is an enthusiastic grower that needs some trimming in late summer.*

LEFT: *Variegated holly adds a touch of colour throughout the year in the area where it grows in front of a camellia.*

Camellias are to be found in all areas of the garden. One of the loveliest of them all is visible from the kitchen as well as the garden.

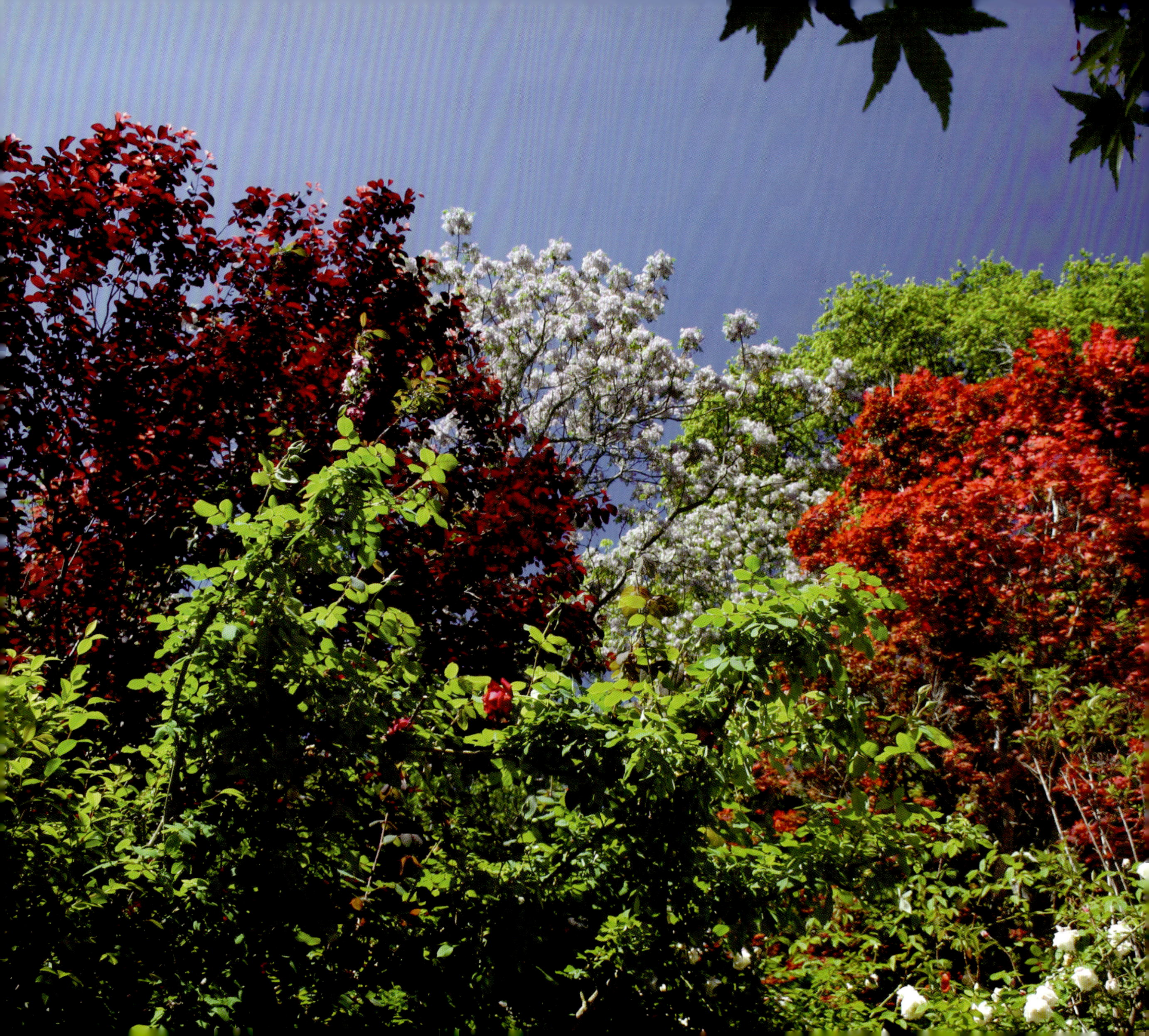

PART 1

THE MILLSTONE TERRACE

For a family enthusiastic about having their meals outdoors as often as possible, the terrain on which the house stood presented a problem. There was only one small area at the back of the house that was on the same level as the house and this area had no trees to shade it.

It was necessary therefore to make a level terrace on the north-western side where the oldest oak stood, spreading its far-flung branches to shade the area near the entrance to the dining room. The area beneath the shade of the oak was about a metre below the level of the stoep, which meant either making steps down to it or else filling in the area to make it the same height as the stoep. Carrying trays laden with food down steps did not appeal to me, so we embarked on the far more time-consuming task of moving soil from the steep slope above to create an area measuring 17 by 13 metres on the same level as the stoep. Here we have lunch all through the hot months. The walls of the house shelter it from the worst of the summer winds. The millstone garden, so called because its table is an old millstone, is easily accessible from the dining room, and is used a great deal for *al fresco* meals throughout the year.

Because most of the garden is far below the level of the house, I tend to plant rare plants, that is plants that are difficult to find in a nursery, near the house so that I can more easily ensure that they are watered thoroughly during dry periods of the year.

The first camellias I planted 60 years ago were on this then new terrace. There are now eight of them, which enhance this area all through autumn and winter. During other seasons their lustrous leaves make a fine background to the smaller plants growing at their feet. We also planted two beautiful Japanese tree maples and four of the type that are shrub-size. Here, too, is a luculia to add lustre to the scene in autumn, and beside the path linking this garden with the back garden are bluebells in spring and other small plants seldom seen in South African gardens.

The millstone terrace is at its most beautiful in winter when the camellias adorn the trees and the surrounding ground when they fall, and the lovely leaves of the maples make it attractive during the other seasons.

OPPOSITE: *This richly coloured background of trees is the view one has from the millstone terrace. It shows clearly how much the colour of leaves can contribute to the beauty of a garden. The tree in the foreground is a plum-coloured prunus, and the further one is a Japanese maple* (Acer japonicum) *whose new leaves emerge translucent ruby-red, become a shade darker in summer and turn scarlet in autumn. The tree behind is an oak and the one with the mauve flowers is a syringa. Roses, red and white, brighten the lower foreground.*

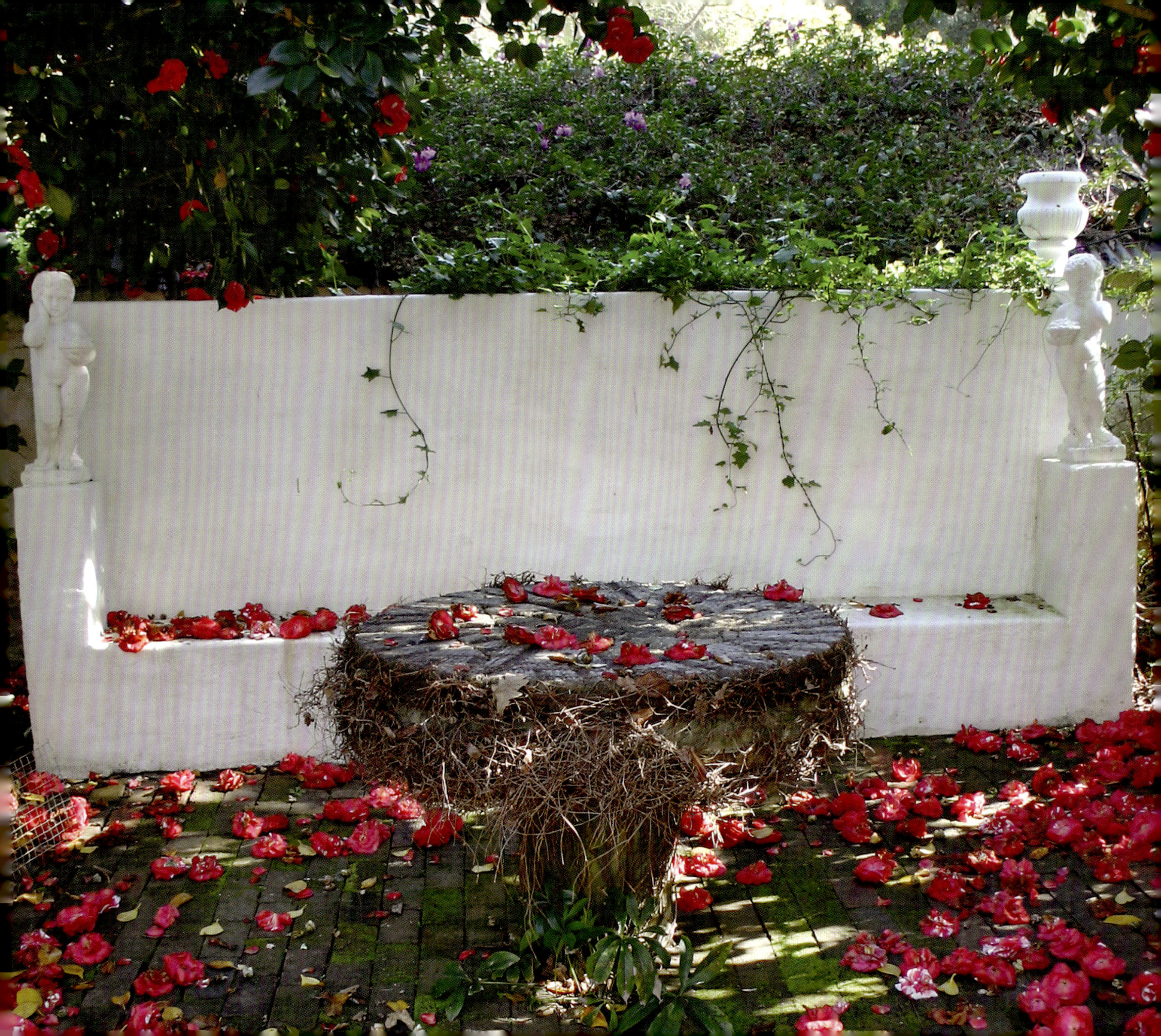

ABOVE: *In summer the leaves of Virginia creeper give the table a decorative edging and the bougainvillaea trained over the roof of the garage makes a colourful background.*

OPPOSITE: *The lovely flowers of camellias cover the table and carpet the ground on the millstone terrace all winter through. The high-backed bench was made to hide the garage and its roof is now hidden by a bougainvillaea. (For notes on the growing of camellias, see the chapter on Winter.)*

94

ABOVE: *Because of the rather dense shade in this garden, only shade-loving plants can be grown. Impatiens add colour to the area in summer.*

RIGHT: *A small maple in a container draped with a low-growing spur flower.*

OPPOSITE PAGE

TOP LEFT: *In spring white azaleas in the deep shade near the bole of the oak lighten the shadow and bring animation to the scene.*

TOP RIGHT: *In mid-spring a lilac-coloured rhododendron I planted about 50 years ago flaunts its beauty between the entrance to the dining room and this terrace. It partially shades the millstone garden and is itself shaded by an ancient oak.*

BOTTOM LEFT: *The shrubby Japanese maple is a slow-growing plant, but its exquisite foliage makes it one of the most ornamental plants for gardens large and small and for growing in a container on a shady patio.*

BOTTOM RIGHT: *The tree form of the Japanese maple is elegant in outline and striking in late autumn and early winter when its pretty leaves turn colour.*

ABOVE: *Justicia is a quick-growing shrub from Brazil that wears a decorative crown of dusty-pink flowers for much of summer. It prefers dappled to deep shade.*

LEFT: *A young camellia nods down on an old azalea in a benign fashion.*

OPPOSITE LEFT: *When winter comes, this area is bright with the flowers of camellias that show up magnificently against their deep-green leaves. These are close-up pictures of two camellias planted 60 years ago that are now four metres tall.*

OPPOSITE RIGHT: *This solitary climbing red rose grows where the shade is lighter to add colour and fragrance to the scene in spring.*

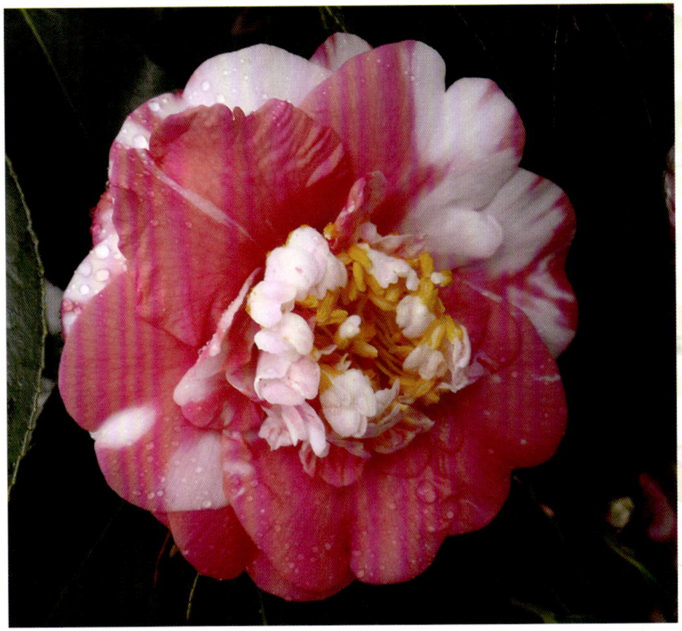

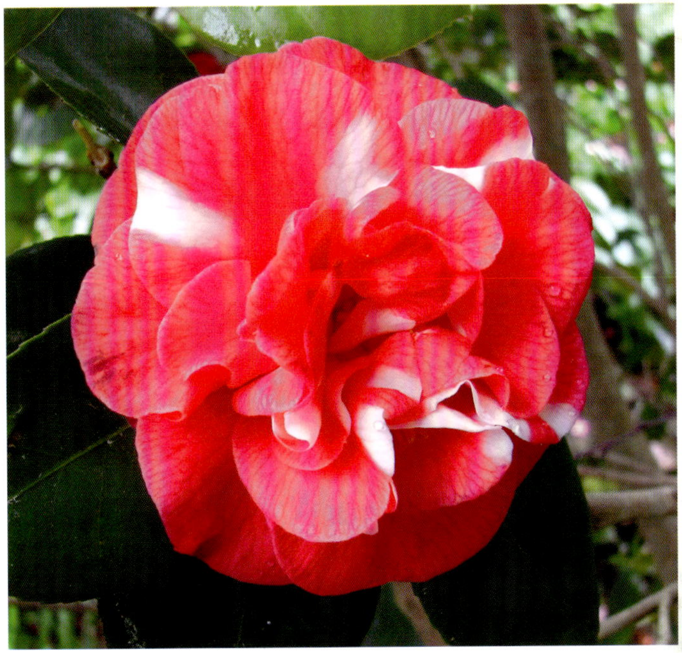

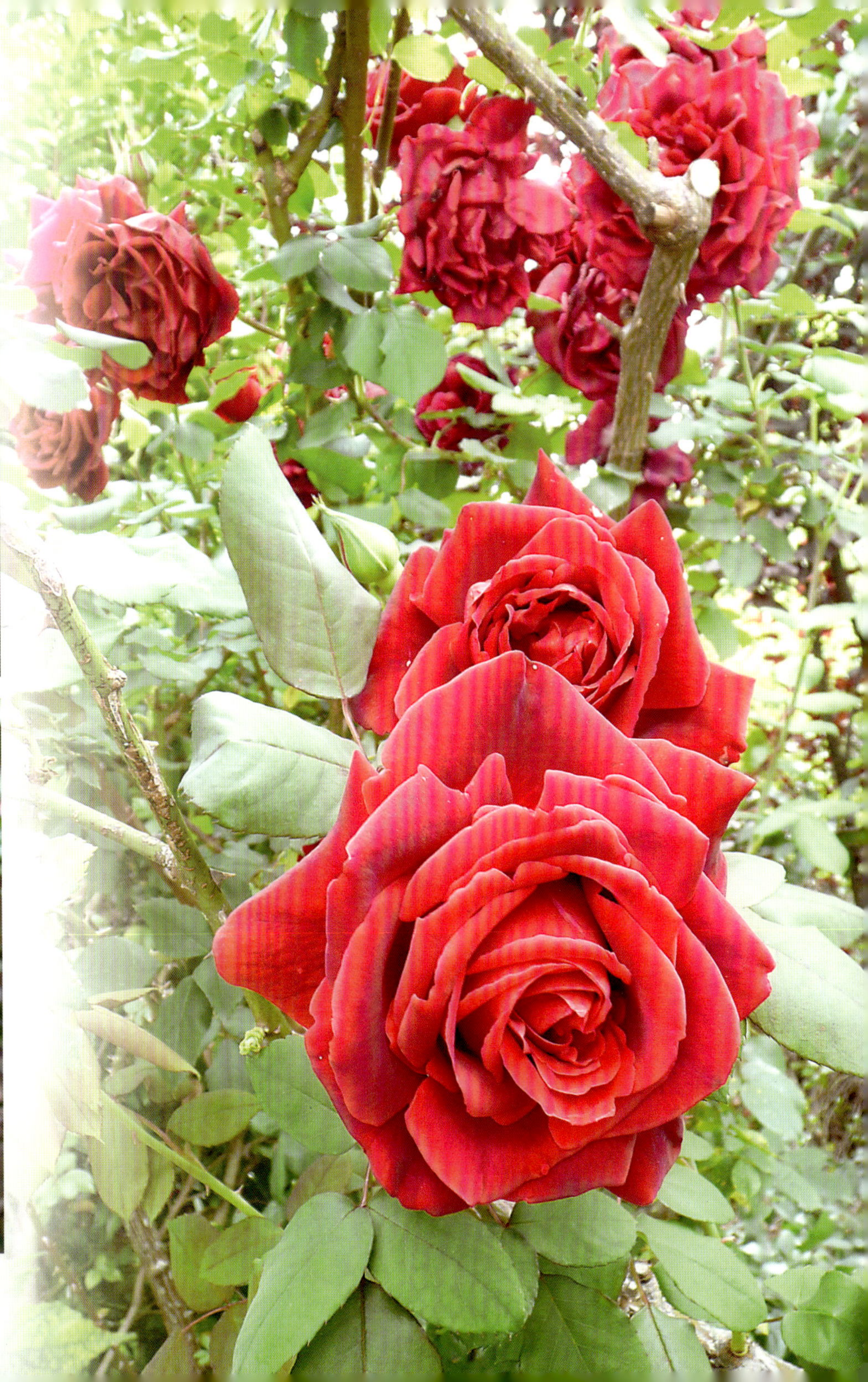

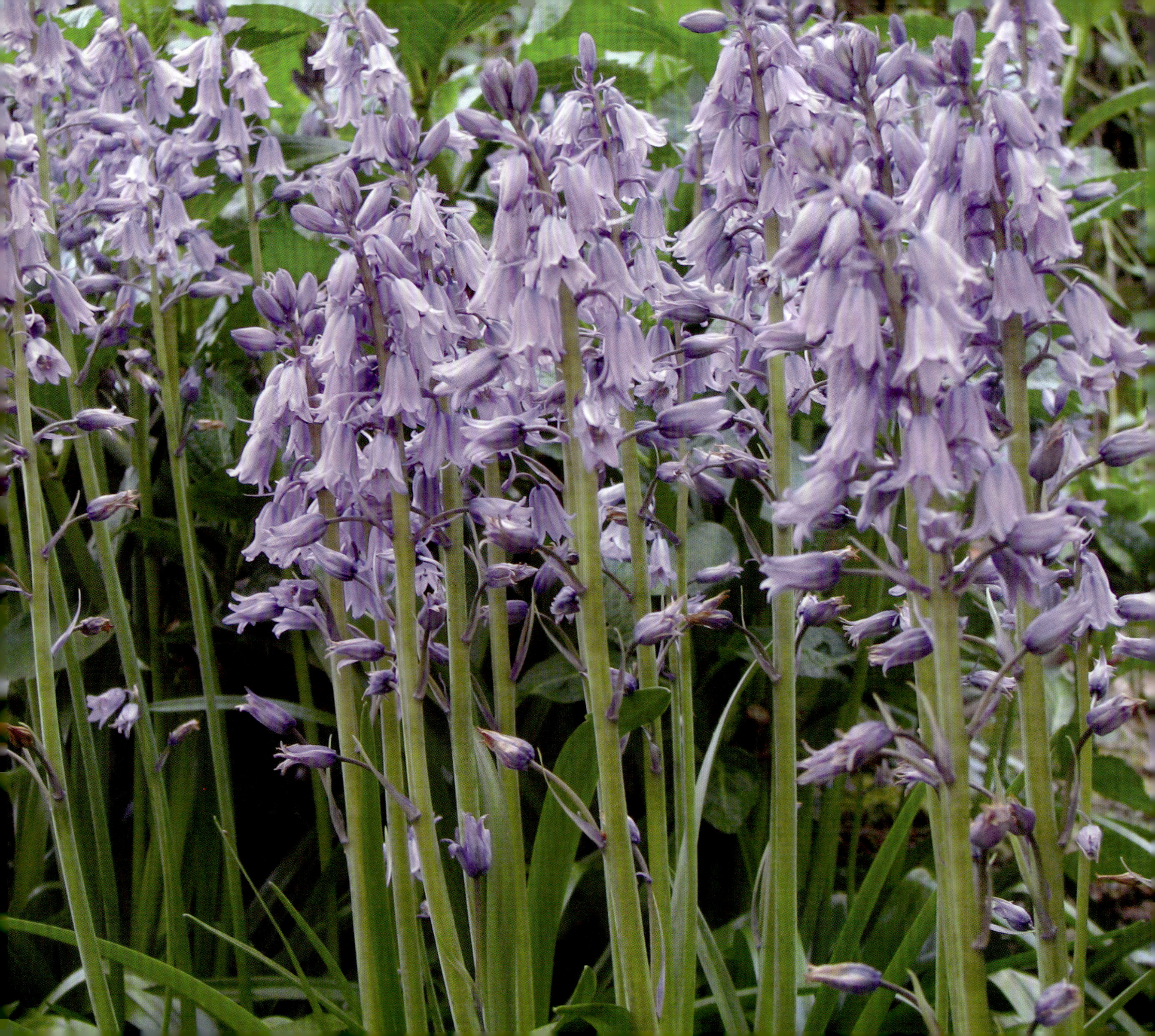

ABOVE AND RIGHT: *Luculia is one of my favourite flowers. The plant itself is rather straggly, but the globular heads of flowers are beautiful and each floret is an exquisite treasure. In addition, its rich perfume pervades both the house and the garden.*

OPPOSITE: *Beneath the maples, bluebells make a pretty picture early in spring.*

PART 11

THE FOUR SEASONS

In this section, I have listed and described the plants I have grown and enjoy at Old Nectar.

They are arranged and described in alphabetical order under the season in which they are most decorative. A few appear in two seasons as they have beautiful flowers in spring or summer and colourful foliage in autumn or winter.

I decided on this arrangement as everyone wants their home

surroundings to be beautiful all the year round, but few people know when the different plants are at their best and most gardening books do not list plants under their season of greatest attraction.

I have used the more friendly common names of the plants and have given their botanical names in the index.

The pictures indicate how colourful the garden is in autumn and winter, but those living in regions where winters are mild will not have this wonderful change in the colours of the leaves before they drop as the plants need cold to cause this brilliant show.

For leaf colour those living in a region where the winter is mild should choose from plants with colourful leaves. These are mostly evergreen plants.

The pictures on these two pages show how dramatic is the change in appearance of the front garden from season to season.

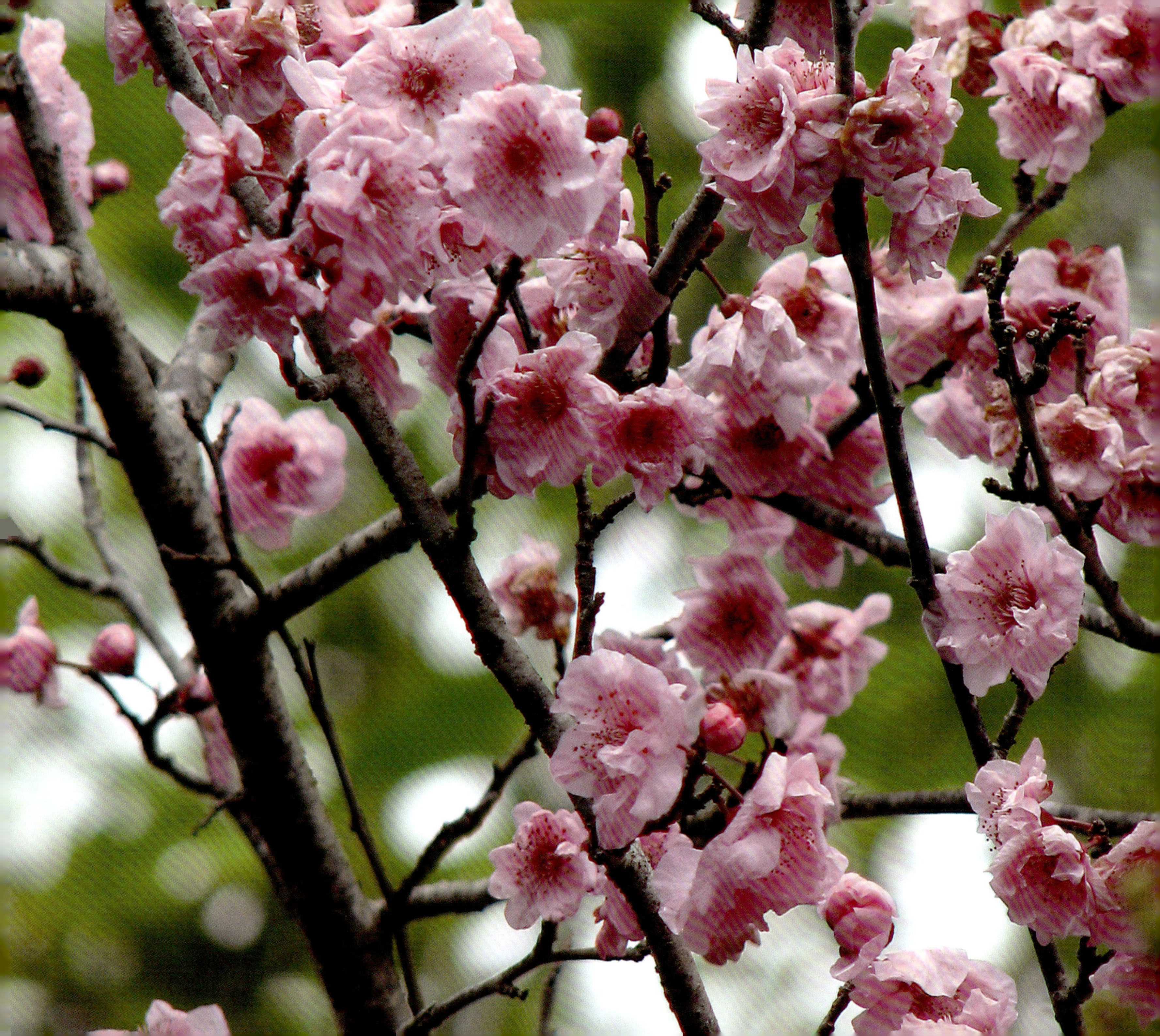

PART 11

SPRING

> For, lo! The winter is past, the rain is over and gone;
> the flowers appear on the earth;
> the time of the singing of birds is come,
> and the voice of the turtle dove is heard in our land.
> – Song of Solomon 2: 11, 12

In the Western Cape spring is really a glory to behold, and it is not surprising that visitors from around the globe come to our country to see and enjoy the endless fields of wild flowers. Like autumn, spring is vibrant and exciting. Even in a small garden there are changes from day to day.

Many years ago a German scientist, Rudolf Marloth, referred to as the Father of South African Botany, named this area the Cape Floral Kingdom. It is not a vast area, a strip extending from Table Mountain north to the Orange River and east towards Port Elizabeth – roughly 1,000 kilometres long by 150 kilometres wide. But one does not have to travel beyond the Cape Peninsula itself, where there are about 2,500 different species to be seen. In the number of species per square kilometre the Cape flora is one of the richest in the world.

From the early 18th century, plant collectors from Europe have visited this country to learn about our plants, to collect seeds and to propagate them. Many of them have been used to ornament gardens in other countries for two centuries. In spring, in Europe and the United States, millions upon millions of plants derived from our wild pelargoniums are grown to enhance window boxes and pots, and countless others can be seen in gardens abroad.

Early in July I start planning and reserving accommodation for the three to four nights I spend in areas north of Cape Town during late August and early September, on a visit to see wild flowers in their natural habitat. The number of visitors is large and there are not many places where overnight accommodation is available, so reserving a room is essential.

In some areas one comes across hectares of brilliant colour – orange, or orange, yellow and mauve combined. A walk into the veld is always rewarding as one then finds hidden in the swathes of colour many very beautiful small plants to delight the eye and inspire the spirit.

Most of these indigenous plants are sun-lovers and do best in friable, gritty or sandy soil. They require a little water only between May and October. As many of them stand fairly severe frost, it is surprising that so few South Africans use these colourful plants to enhance their gardens. On a visit to Australia and New Zealand 35 years ago, packets of seeds and also bulbs of many of these plants were on sale at nurseries and

OPPOSITE: *The ornamental plum (prunus) is an ideal tree for the small garden as its bronze leaves are colourful for nine months of the year and the masses of pretty, dainty flowers appear before its new spring leaves. It is hardy to all but extreme frost and, once well-grown, will survive long periods with little water.*

garden shops there, whereas here, the country of their origin, one had difficulty finding a source of supply and there is still comparatively little interest shown in growing these veld flowers.

When I started gardening I planted beds of our wild flowers and enjoyed their willingness to grow and their enchanting flowers. Of the spring-flowering bulbs my favourites were the sparaxis with their gaily coloured faces, the lachenalias with waxy flowers mostly of delicate pastel shades, and ixias, with dancing butterfly-like flowers on long slender stems. However, as the trees in the garden grew so did the area of shade, and the space once filled by these native bulbs is now covered by shade-loving ground covers.

The month of September is a vibrant time, with every plant surging ahead trying to outdo its neighbours. It's generally cool and wet and there are not many days when one can linger long in the garden to enjoy the rapid change that takes place day by day. Indeed, one can often notice a change in size and shape in the unfurling of the leaves of the trees and shrubs between the morning and afternoon. Some start their new growth earlier in spring than do others. By the end of September the oaks and magnolias are in full leaf whereas the poplars and elms show no signs of leaf growth and others – the copper beech, liquidambar and viburnums – are festooned with tiny fresh leaves.

They vary also in their flowering time. Every year the almond is the first to captivate one with its delightful starry white flowers so delicately arranged against the dark stems. Then come the flowers of the ornamental plum – pale pink to rose. As they fade it pushes out its gleaming new bronze leaves. The ornamental peach follows to colour the scene. I have one spectacular, 50-year-old tree which delights all who pass by. It was propagated at a time when nurserymen were plant-lovers and took pride in producing plants of great beauty. In this case the nurseryman grafted three different colours – white, pale pink and rose – on to the same rootstock. What years of pleasure this tree has brought me and so many others! I remember photographing it 40 years ago with a new daughter-in-law dressed in royal blue standing beneath it. She is now a grandmother. The great thing about living in a garden of trees is that as one grows older in appearance and becomes less active, the trees grow larger and more beautiful!

Before the ornamental peach has shed its lovely mantle, the crabapples start producing their charming blossoms – delicately formed and of soft shades of pink to rose. Finally the Japanese cherry, named Kanzan, steals the show. It is my favourite, not only because of its glorious canopy of clusters of double, pink flowers but because of its silky patterned bark and its splendid winter colour. I have four other named cultivars but they are not as beautiful.

Many years ago these highly ornamental trees were hybridised from those grown for fruit, and they are ideal trees to grow in small gardens as well as large ones. I would like to see the streets of our towns and villages lined with these ornamental trees.

Week by week during September the exquisite leaves of the Japanese maples charm one as they slowly unfurl, just a tiny fraction, each day. By the end of the month they are in full leaf – the green types a translucent green and those with bronze leaves having a burnished appearance. The chorisia is also a lovely sight at this time of the year as its new lustrous bronze leaves show up well against the sky. The syringa, festooned with its pale-yellow berries, and the shrubby magnolia with purple flowers also contribute colour to the scene. There are now fewer flowers on the camellias but still enough to make a pleasing show. The different types have provided five months of colour. It is the azaleas that highlight my garden in early-to-mid spring. They like the acid soil, the shade and the regular watering provided by our winter rain just before and during their flowering period. There are thousands of different named cultivars and, each year sees the introduction of new ones. The hardiest are the old mauve and white ones that were the only type available when I arrived at Old Nectar. They have a faint, sweet scent which adds to their charm. Azaleas are delightful flowers for arrangements, not only because of their shape and colours, but because they last a long time when picked.

At this season of the year, when the roses are putting out their tender new shoots and leaves, the insects are standing by ready to attack. I do a circuit of the garden twice a day to deal with them: at ten in the morning and just after afternoon tea. The aphids are seldom a bother. Because we rarely use insecticides we have ladybirds, which seem to be able to deal with the aphids. The first of the large insects to appear are the stinkbugs, which chew up the tips of the rose shoots at an alarming rate. Then come the voracious, insatiable larger pests – mammoth beetles in gaily spotted or striped jerseys. If one deals with them immediately, they do not get a chance to proliferate. I pick them off by hand.

More damage is done in the rose garden through disease than is ever done by insect pests. It will generally be found that the insect pests are seasonal. They appear for a certain length of time, do some damage, and then disappear. Diseases, on the other hand, go from bad to worse, and many plants may be destroyed before the disease is detected. It is important, therefore, to learn to recognise diseases so that they can be taken in hand before too much damage is done, and it is better still, of course, to prevent outbreaks of disease. The most serious diseases which attack rose bushes are fungus diseases. They originate from spores which are spread by insects, rain, and wind. They may be in the soil undetected for some time before they become evident on plants. If left to develop, they will in time kill the plants. Heat plus humidity favours their development, and in spring and summer, gardeners should be on the qui vive for outbreaks of these diseases, and are advised to apply preventive sprays from the beginning of spring. The most devastating of fungus diseases are black spot, rust and mildew. In areas of summer rains these diseases appear with the rains.

Here black spot usually manifests itself in spring and early summer. When it becomes evident, it has already got into the plant body. No time should be wasted before applying treatment. It appears as circular, purplish-black spots which show up on the leaves, usually the lower ones. The spots increase in size and the leaves begin to drop off. If defoliation is allowed to continue, the plant will be left without means of assimilating food and will eventually die. The spores in the meanwhile are infecting the entire garden. They winter in the soil, and it is important to spray both the bushes and the soil. To prevent the spread of the disease, spray regularly once every seven to ten days during periods of warm, rainy weather, applying the spray to the undersides of the leaves as well as the top. Horticultural stores sell different sprays efficacious against black spot and rust. Rust appears as brilliant, orange-coloured, powdery spots on the undersides of the leaves. Young stems may also be attacked. Much the same treatment must be used as is recommended for black spot.

The earliest symptom of mildew is the appearance of a whitish, powdery coating on the tips of young leaves and shoots. When the disease is established, the leaves appear to be almost completely white and they curl up. As in other plant diseases which attack the leaves, the entire health of the plant is impaired, as the reduced leaf-surface cannot convert enough of the food material absorbed by the roots into assimilable food to keep the plants robust and vigorous. To prevent the spread of mildew, we spray with a recommended fungicide or dust with dusting-sulphur. Two or three applications may be necessary to clear up the infection. It is a simple operation and takes little time. Put a handful or two of dusting-sulphur in an old sock and shake it so that the sulphur settles on the leaves. It is advisable to do the sulphur-dusting early in the morning as the slight dampness of the leaves at that time of day makes the dust cling better. Plants should not be dusted during intensely hot weather as the action of hot sunshine on the sulphur may scorch the leaves.

If a disease has made its appearance, it is not enough to spray and dust once only as the spores are developing in the ground and will attack the plant again within a short period. Three or more applications of a dust or spray is the best way of combating a disease. If this sounds like a lot of bother, remember that this attention will keep the roses in good health and produce flowers until the end of autumn, or longer.

Roses tend to bear an abundance of flowers during their first flush in spring, and later in spring there are very few flowers on the plants. Some years ago I found that cutting off fading flowers on a thousand plants every day was an onerous task. I therefore decided to reduce the number of early blooms by removing some of the shoots before the buds developed. I now have a wonderful show of roses in mid-spring

ABOVE: *The Australian frangipani has leaves which remain attractive throughout the year, and when its clusters of yellow-shaded flowers appear the scent pervades large areas of the garden. Recommended for large and small gardens where frosts are not extreme.*

ABOVE LEFT: *Azaleas are decorative plants for gardens large and small as they make a glorious show in early-to-mid spring. There are many thousands of hybrids with flowers of different colours and combinations of colour. We have about 200 plants, but a single plant in a large pot or in the garden is a joyous introduction to spring. Azaleas need shade and acid soil and most large nurseries now stock the right compost to promote their growth. In areas with dry winters, they should also be watered regularly through winter and spring. Some of those in the garden here are now 50 years old. They have never been given any fertiliser or compost other than that put in the holes in which they were planted. Because they are now more than a metre high and wide, we try to keep them from becoming taller by cutting off two or three stems on each plant about 30 cm above the ground, immediately after they have finished flowering. This promotes new growth low down where we made the cut. Azaleas enjoy cool-to-cold conditions.*

LEFT: *This golden azalea is different from the other azaleas inasmuch as it is deciduous whereas they are evergreen and it flowers when most of the others have finished flowering.*

and also in later spring. The operation is quick and easy. In early to late September one simply cuts or pinches off with one's fingers 10–15 cm of the tender tips of some of the shoots where buds are just forming. I generally remove about one third of these shoots on mature plants. On young roses one would pinch out fewer.

There are only three climbers to highlight the first month of spring. One is the wisteria. It makes a fine show in the pergola and near the house where there is another one growing into a crabapple, which flowers at the same time. It has the most enchanting scent that drifts far and wide. As soon as the scent becomes strong, there appear, like magic, large bumble bees about 4 cm long and almost half as wide. They dart around at great speed collecting nectar from the flowers. The remarkable thing is that one never sees a young bee. They appear fully grown and, as soon as the flowers begin to fade, they disappear. I assume that it is the scent of the wisteria, and only the wisteria, that attracts them as they are never seen near any other scented plants. Another September-flowering climber that brings joy is a sulphur-yellow banksia rose. Very exuberant it is, even though rarely watered. The third climber is the sweetly scented jasmine, a plant that has many attributes – pretty glossy leaves, delightful ivory-white flowers with a sweet, pervasive scent, and a willingness to grow even when seldom watered. In my garden it needs cutting back hard, once a year.

Of the shrubs, the first to flower in September – and one of my favourites – is the Cape may. It effervesces with a profusion of arching stems covered with clusters of white flowers. It's a graceful plant and decorative even when it is not in flower. Another early spring-flowering shrub is philadelphus, commonly known as mock orange because the scent of its flowers is rather like that of orange blossom. A richly rewarding shrub for early-to-mid spring is eupatorium, sometimes referred to as giant ageratum, as the flowers are reminiscent of those of the ground-hugging ageratum. It grows fast and should be cut back once a year to limit its spread. It has large, attractive, velvety leaves and huge heads of small flowers of a rich mauve hue, which the bees love. It stands some cold but not frosty conditions. Flowering at the same time is the Mexican orange blossom (choisya). It has neat, lustrous foliage and clusters of starry, white, five-petalled flowers with a faint scent of orange blossom, which accounts for its common name. It too will, when once established, perform well.

The bluebells I planted six years ago have multiplied at an incredible rate and in an incredible fashion. I planted a few bulbs in a row near a jet water line under the shade of a maple and near the house so that I could easily ensure that the water jets in that area were working properly. I assumed that the plants would multiply only in the area that received water, but they have done the opposite. They have spread further and further away from the watered area and are now flourishing in a dry area where even weeds do not grow. They make a splendid show all through September. I wish I had more plants with blue flowers. It is a happy colour. There are forget-me-nots in the pergola and I once grew anchusa, a tall plant with flowers similar to those of forget-me-not. Several times I have planted our charming wild felicia, but it always sulks and then dies away.

Gunnera, the waterside plant along the stream, sends out its new leaves early in spring – the shape and size of a dinner plate, with a crinkled surface. By summer they measure a metre across. This plant from Chile is a dramatic one for a large water garden.

By the end of September there is a palpable surge on the part of the flowering trees and shrubs to speed up the flowering process. The first to demand admiration at this time of the year is the venerable pear. It is well over a hundred years old and produces a full head of creamy-white blossom – determined not to be outshone by the neighbouring, much younger trees. The ivory colour of the flowers is a splendid foil to the deep-bronze new leaves of the copper beech. Nearby, the flowers of the Australian frangipani give off an alluring scent. They are produced in clusters and are sulphur-yellow in colour. The glossy leaves add to the attraction of this tree, which grows tall but not broad. This is one of the trees that produce flowers for a long time. Nearby is a horse chestnut tree with its conical heads of flowers.

At this time, too, the myriad of flowers produced by the climbing

LEFT: *This group of azaleas, planted 50 years ago, is next to the house. Its brightly coloured flowers bring a sparkle to the scene in the grey days we have in early spring.*

RIGHT: *Bluebells are seldom seen in South African gardens. Here they grow and multiply very well. The shade of high trees suits them best. They tolerate extremes of frost and long periods with little or no water. They do, however, need to be watered from late autumn to spring.*

rose, crepuscule, appear. This rose was first introduced a century ago. Because it is the only climbing rose I know that flowers on and off during the year and not only in spring, I have planted it in different areas of the garden.

The last two to three weeks of October are the most colourful of the year – with the rose garden in full flower and the following trees, shrubs and climbers also in flower; the late-flowering azaleas, bignonia, brunfelsia, cherries, clematis, geraniums, honeysuckle, hymenosporum, irises, murraya, nasturtium, petrea, rhododendron, snowball and the syringa.

The attractive flowers of brunfelsia, which range in shades of mauve to white, have a delightful scent as do those of the murraya, which is native to the East Indies. Its cup-shaped, five-petalled flowers resemble those of orange blossom in appearance and scent and its dark-green, glossy oval leaflets are pretty throughout the year. Petrea, a climber native to Mexico, is seldom seen in Cape gardens. I have succeeded in growing only one against a sun-washed, sheltering wall. It is now over 30 years old and makes a grand display every year. The two plants of snowball (viburnum) in the front garden put on a most impressive show in mid-spring when they bear their large round globes of cream-coloured flowers and again in winter when their foliage turns brilliant shades of bronze to crimson. Clematis is one of my favourite climbers despite the fact that it is unpredictable in growth. The flowers are so enchanting that the extra attention they require is worth while. There are hundreds of named cultivars, some with small flowers, generally known as *Clematis montana*, and others with large flowers carried on slender, fragile stems. They do best in regions with temperate to cold winters and should be planted where their roots are in shade and their top-growth gets sun. Mine are on the south side of pillars in the pergola. They tend to die back during the summer when the air is dry and brittle, no matter how much water is applied to their roots.

In November at the northern end of the pergola the paulownia, a flowering tree from China, bears its handsome, pyramidal panicles of flowers, rather like those of a foxglove in form and shaded pale to deep amethyst. Unfortunately, because I planted it too near a towering oak, the tree has become contorted in growth. Would that there was a nursery in the country that could supply me with another plant to grow in a more favourable spot.

Decorating one of the pillars of the pergola, near the paulownia, is an exuberant climber known as sky flower (thunbergia). It has heart-shaped leaves as much as 15 cm in length and produces cascades of lilac flowers rather like those of a gloxinia in shape. It is native to India and does best where frosts are not severe. We cut the plant back to half-size when flowering is over.

Brunfelsia wears its mantle of flowers, which change in colour from day to day, in mid-spring. It is worth growing for the delightful scent of the flowers. It is native to Brazil and, although it will tolerate mild frost, it does best where frost does not occur. It does well in coastal gardens.

ABOVE: *A close-up of the single flowers of Cape may. There is also a hybrid with double flowers.*

TOP: *Cantua is a quick-growing shrub, straggly in habit, and best planted at the back of a shrub border. The flowers of a rich cyclamen shade festoon the plant early in spring. In inland gardens, plant it where it is shaded from the hot afternoon sun. It is hardy only to moderate frost.*

LEFT: *Bulbine. Different species of this plant grow wild in many parts of South Africa. The leaves are succulent and the plant has tuberous fleshy roots that enable it to stand long periods of drought. It produces pretty flowers in cone-shaped heads on stems about 45 cm tall. Bulbine grows in poor soil and in full sun or light shade and makes a good ground cover where water is in short supply. The sap from the leaves is efficacious in treating sores or abrasions.*

I can think of no lovelier sight than the ornamental cherry named Kanzan in mid-spring when it becomes festooned with lovely globules of pale-pink blossom. There are many other named cherries, but this is my favourite. I should like to see it planted as a street tree in all the towns with cool-to-cold winter and a reasonable rainfall.

112

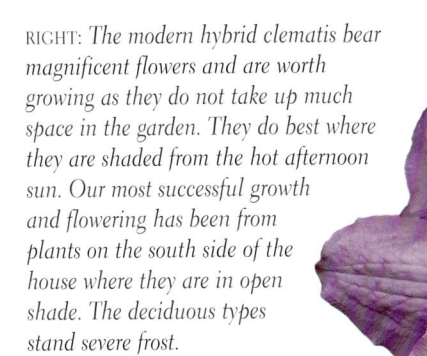

RIGHT: *The modern hybrid clematis bear magnificent flowers and are worth growing as they do not take up much space in the garden. They do best where they are shaded from the hot afternoon sun. Our most successful growth and flowering has been from plants on the south side of the house where they are in open shade. The deciduous types stand severe frost.*

FAR RIGHT: *Columbines have the grace of ballerinas. The first ones we planted were the exotic hybrids with large handsome flowers of unusual colours. These seeded very well but the resulting flowers were those of Shakespeare's day. I find them more attractive than the giant hybrids and they have now found their way to all the shady parts of the garden where their fern-like leaves cover the ground for much of the year.*

OPPOSITE PAGE:

TOP LEFT: *The first shrub to gladden the garden in spring is Cape may. Not only does it produce masses of lovely white flowers, but it stands our hot, very dry summers without flinching. It also endures severe frost and survives on little water. The plants in the drive are in the shade of trees. They are never watered and they continue to grow and flower as well each spring as those planted in full sun. Mature plants should be cut back by a third to a half after flowering is over to keep them from becoming large and straggly.*

TOP RIGHT: *Cerastium is a charming, ground-hugging plant with a dense arrangement of tiny silvery leaves that make a neat carpet on the ground. In spring it carries a mass of dainty, five-petalled flowers to embellish the picture. It is hardy to frost but needs a weekly watering during dry periods.*

BOTTOM LEFT: *Choisya is a very attractive shrub that flowers when those of the Cape may are fading. Its delightful glossy foliage makes a good background to its white scented flowers. It stands frost but should be watered regularly.*

BOTTOM RIGHT: *This clematis with smaller flowers, known as Clematis montana, bears many more flowers than the large-flowering cultivars, grows more vigorously and makes an impressive show.*

ABOVE: *Crinum grow wild in many parts of South Africa. The trumpet-shaped flowers of some of them make an impressive show. Crinum bulbispermum, sometimes referred to as the Orange River lily, because it was first found there, produces its flowers in mid-spring. It will grow in frosty gardens.*

ABOVE LEFT: *The crabapple is a good shade tree to plant in the small as well as large garden as it can be trimmed in winter to reduce its size should it begin to outgrow the space available. The charming white, pink or rose-coloured flowers are followed by attractive bunches of miniature crimson fruit in summer and autumn. It is hardy to very severe frost and, once established, will endure fairly long periods with little water.*

LEFT: *Erigeron is a small, tufty plant which will turn itself into a ground cover in no time as it scatters its seed far and wide. I let it grow only to soften the front steps and in a couple of other places that are seldom watered. It has to be weeded out from time to time. It is both drought- and frost-tolerant.*

OPPOSITE: *Day lily is one of the lily-like plants that thrive and multiply from year to year without receiving much attention. They seem to be able to adapt themselves to any soil and climatic conditions. There are numerous hybrids with semi-double as well as single flowers and of a wide range of colours which include orange, maroon, tawny red, pink and coppery shades. I grow mostly the species which has flowers of bright canary yellow.*

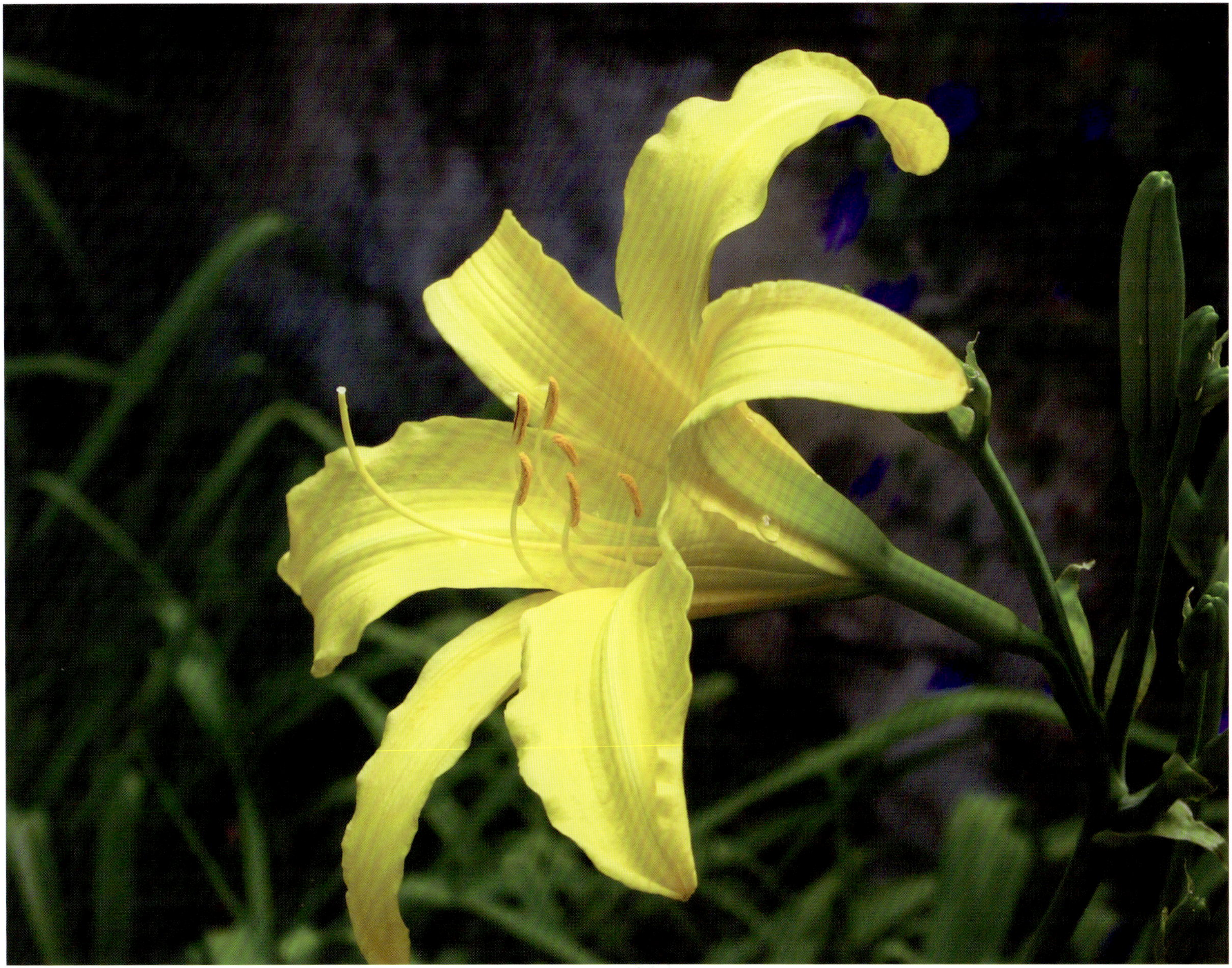

ABOVE: *The giant ageratum (eupatorium) is not recommended for gardens where sharp frosts are experienced. It needs regular watering. This is a very quick-growing plant with large velvety leaves and decorative clusters of mauve flowers. It should be trimmed back after flowering.*

ABOVE LEFT: *Our native geranium is a charming small plant with pretty pale-amethyst flowers. Massed, it makes an attractive ground cover. Here it decorates a crack in the front steps. It is not hardy to much cold and needs to be watered during autumn and winter.*

LEFT: *Honeysuckles grow wild in many parts of the northern hemisphere and there are many species and hybrids. The one most popular in our country is known as Lonicera periclymenum. Its clusters of cream-tinged rose flowers appear in spring and spread their fragrance around. It tolerates frost and long periods with little water.*

OPPOSITE: *Horse chestnut. Its large leaves are decorative for most of the year. The flowers appear in ornamental spikes in spring and have a faint sweet scent. This is a tree for large gardens that have cold winters and a good rainfall.*

117

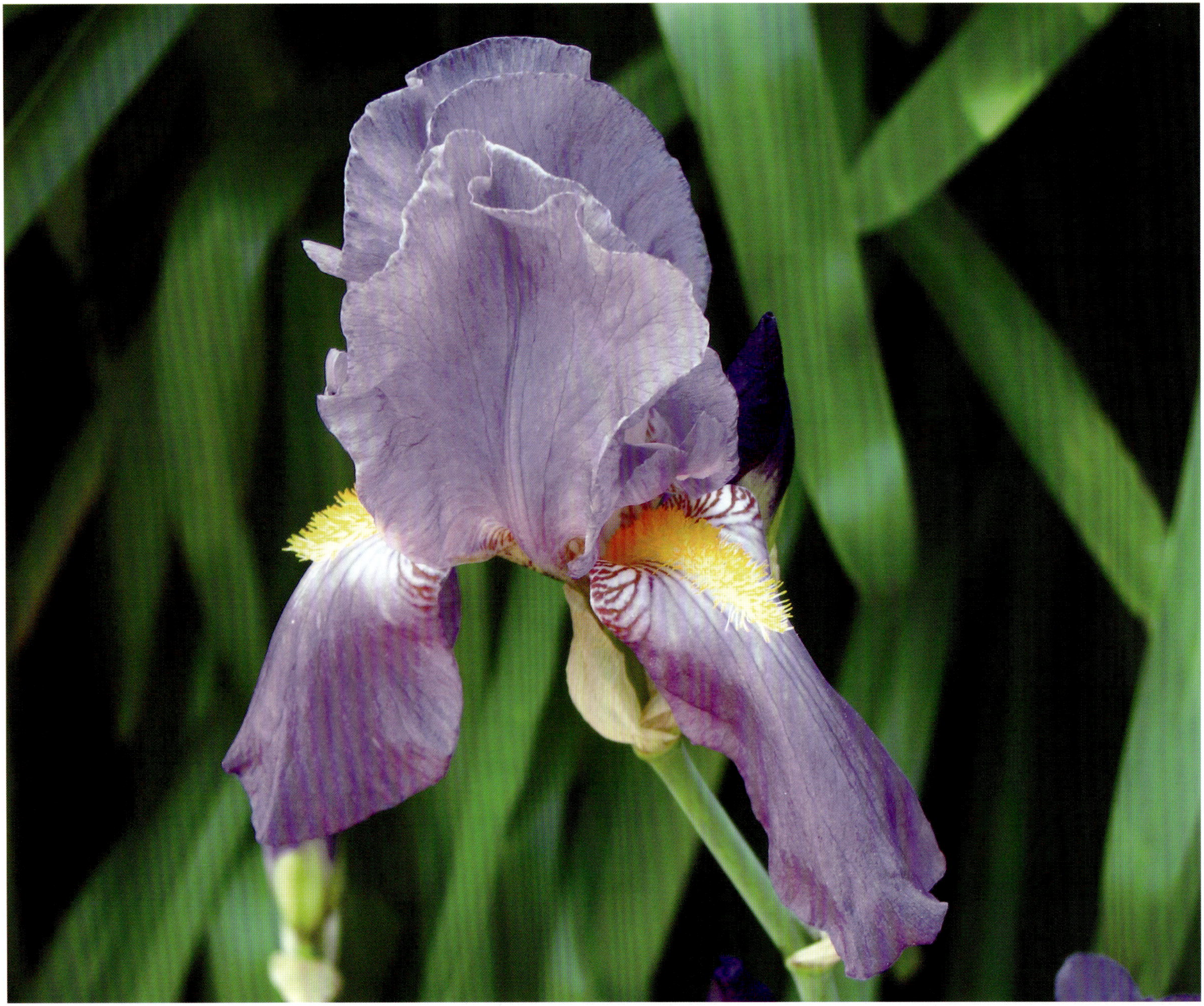

ABOVE: *This iris,* Iris japonica, *is a highly decorative species which sends out dark-green tufts of leaves from which emerge white-to-lavender flowers only 5 cm across with orange markings in the centre and ruffled margins.*

ABOVE LEFT: *Indian hawthorn is an evergreen shrub with leathery leaves. It grows to a metre or two in height and spread but can be kept to a smaller size. Near the coast they do well in full sun, but in hot inland gardens it is a good idea to plant it where it will be shaded from the hot afternoon sun. Stands moderate frost.*

LEFT: *Jasmine. This very-ready-to-grow climber produces a foaming mass of very pretty fragrant flowers that show up well against its neat dark-green glossy leaves. It is native to China and stands considerable frost. It needs to be kept in check by reducing its spread after flowering is over.*

OPPOSITE: *Iris. In myth Iris was a goddess who acted as a messenger of the gods and displayed, as her sign, the rainbow. The bearded iris include all the colours of the rainbow. They stand frost and dryness but need to be lifted and divided every four years to ensure good flowering.*

ABOVE: *Magnolia*. The name includes large shrubs and trees with spectacular flowers. It is necessary to give the botanical names in this case, as common names can be confusing. Magnolia liliiflora *is a species from central China which forms a tall shrub carrying handsome purple flowers in spring. Most magnolias need acid soil enriched with compost and, when established, they stand frost. In hot inland gardens they should be planted in high shade or on the south side of the house.*

OPPOSITE: Magnolia stellata *grows slowly to three metres. This species is a native of Japan. It bears its delightful flowers with reflexed petals in very early spring before the leaves grow out.*

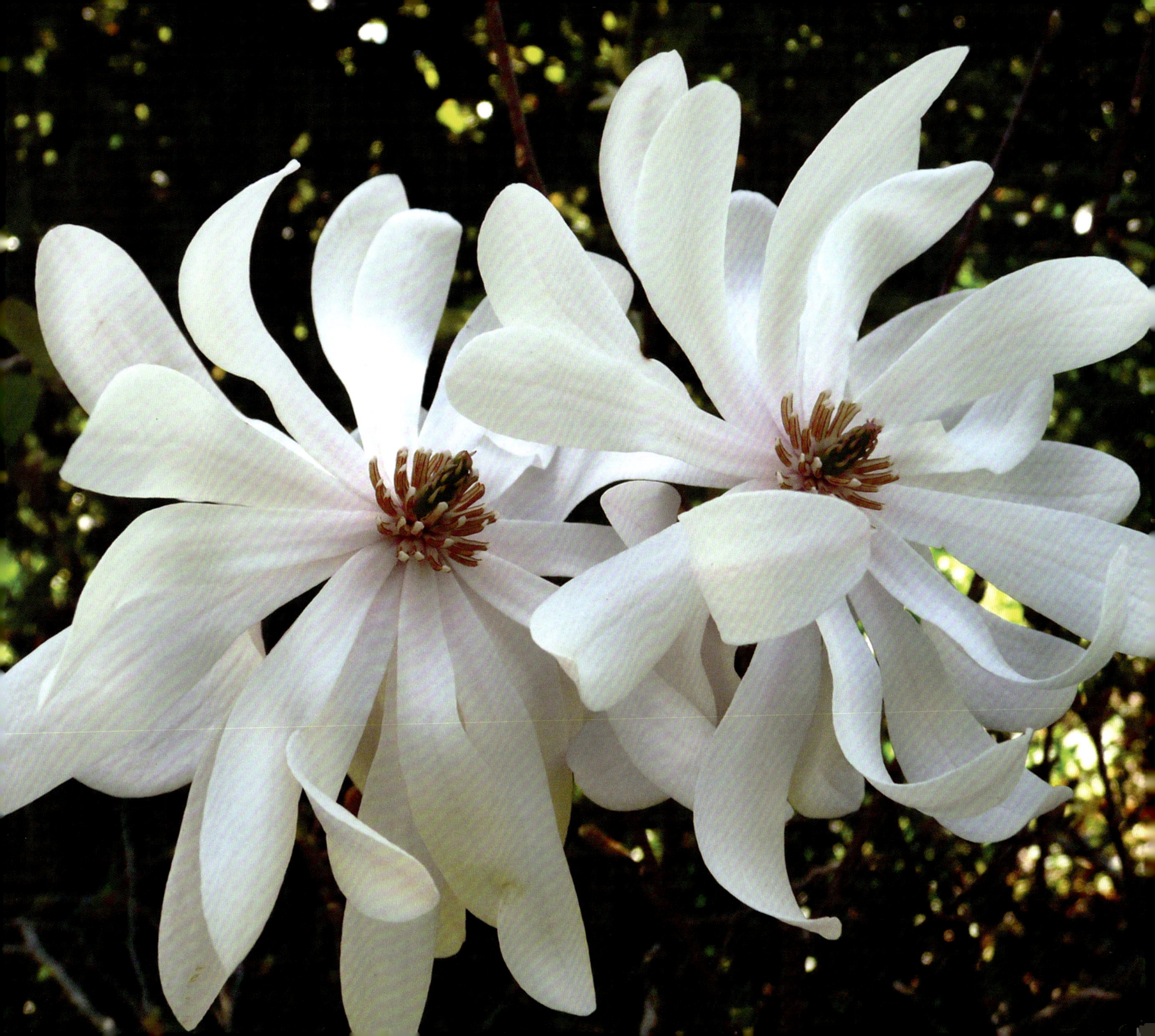

ABOVE: *Moses-in-the-bulrushes* is an attractive waterside plant growing to 30 cm. The colours of the flowers include blue, purple, white and rose. The leaves are slender and curve about the stems.

LEFT: *Leucospermums* are sometimes referred to as pincushion plants. There are many very pretty species for gardens large and small. These plants are to be found growing wild in the south-western Cape. They are not for frosty or dry gardens. Regular watering in autumn and winter is necessary to promote good flowering.

ABOVE: *Murraya.* This pretty shrub from Southeast Asia has glossy dark-green leaves which show up the orange-blossom-like white flowers that give off a sweet perfume in spring. It does best where winters are mild and likes some shade in hot dry areas.

ABOVE RIGHT: *Nasturtiums* are enthusiastic plants – so keen to show off their leaves and flowers that they appear out of the blue and fling themselves joyously around, across paths and over neighbouring plants. The leaves are tasty in sandwiches and salads. They will grow in gardens with frost and they tolerate fairly dry conditions.

RIGHT: *Ochna* is one of the prettiest of our indigenous flowering shrubs. Its glossy green leaves are of ornamental value throughout the year and the clusters of bright-yellow flowers are followed by colourful seedheads in summer. It does best in mild climate areas.

ABOVE: *One seldom finds petrea growing in gardens in the south-western Cape. It is a rangy climber that does best in warm gardens but tolerates moderate frost.*

OPPOSITE: *The flowering peach is excellent for gardens large and small as it can be trimmed to keep it from growing too large. The ornamental flowers, snow-white, pink or rose, highlight the garden early in spring. It is tolerant of cold, and, when well grown, it can survive long periods with little water.*

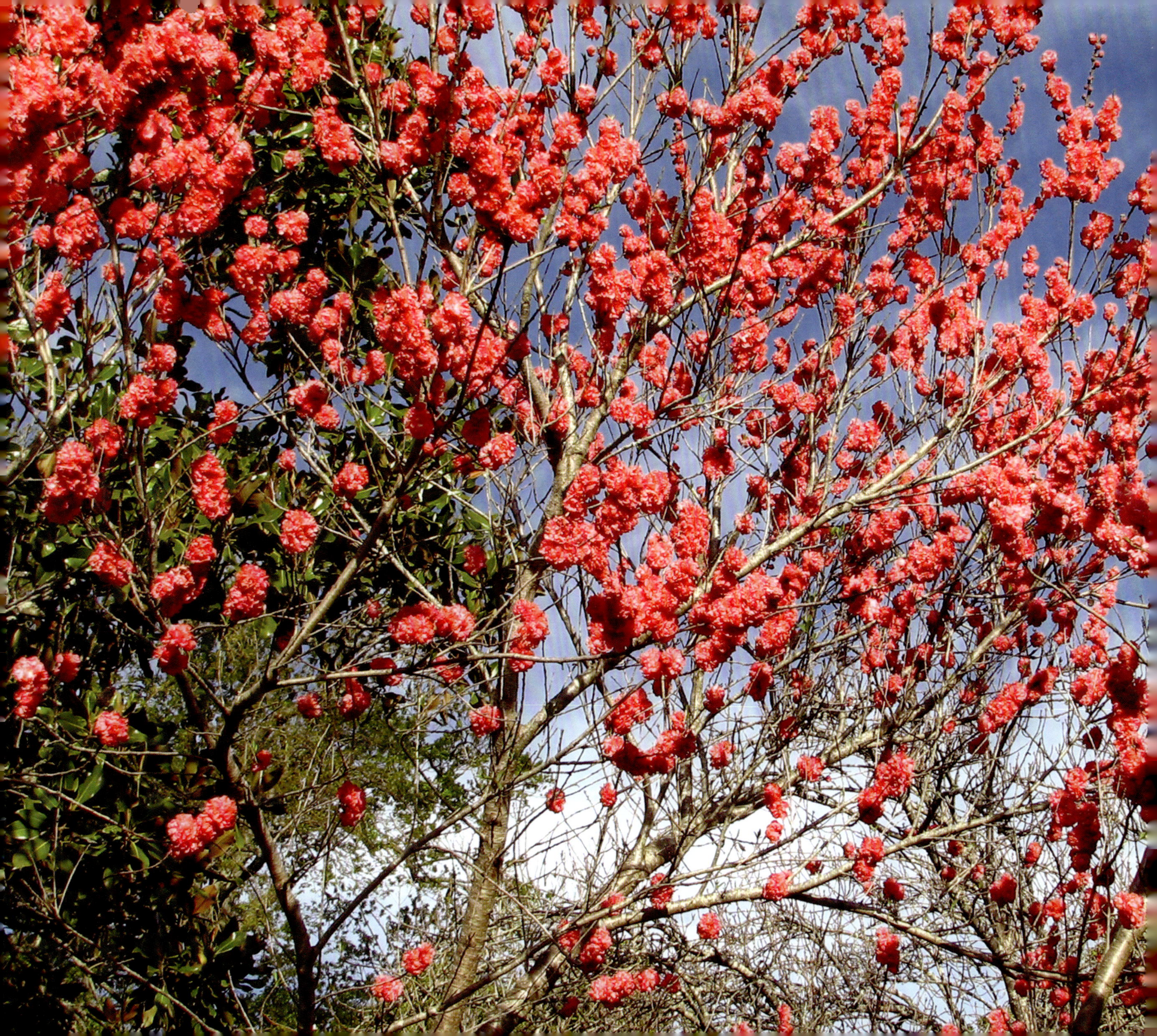

ABOVE: *Philadelphus*, sometimes referred to as mock orange, is an exuberant shrub that flings its arching stems far and wide, the better to display its delightful snow-white flowers. It survives severe winters and will also tolerate summer dryness.

LEFT: The ornamental plum (prunus) is an ideal tree for the small garden as its bronze leaves are colourful for nine months of the year and the masses of pretty, dainty flowers appear before its new spring leaves. It is hardy to all but extreme frost and, once well-grown, will survive long periods with little water.

Privet. There are several types grown as hedges or windbreaks. If not trimmed, they develop into small shade trees. Because of their resistance to both sharp frost and long periods of dryness they are good plants for gardens where such conditions prevail. Here its abundance of ivory-white flowers makes a pleasing foreground to the plum-coloured leaves of a prunus. To keep it to shrub-size, trim it back each year after flowering.

OPPOSITE: Pieris are shrubs and small trees that belong to the heath family. They like acid soil, rich in humus, and do best in regions with a high rainfall. The plant in the garden is a cultivar of *Pieris formosa*, which stands cold conditions well.

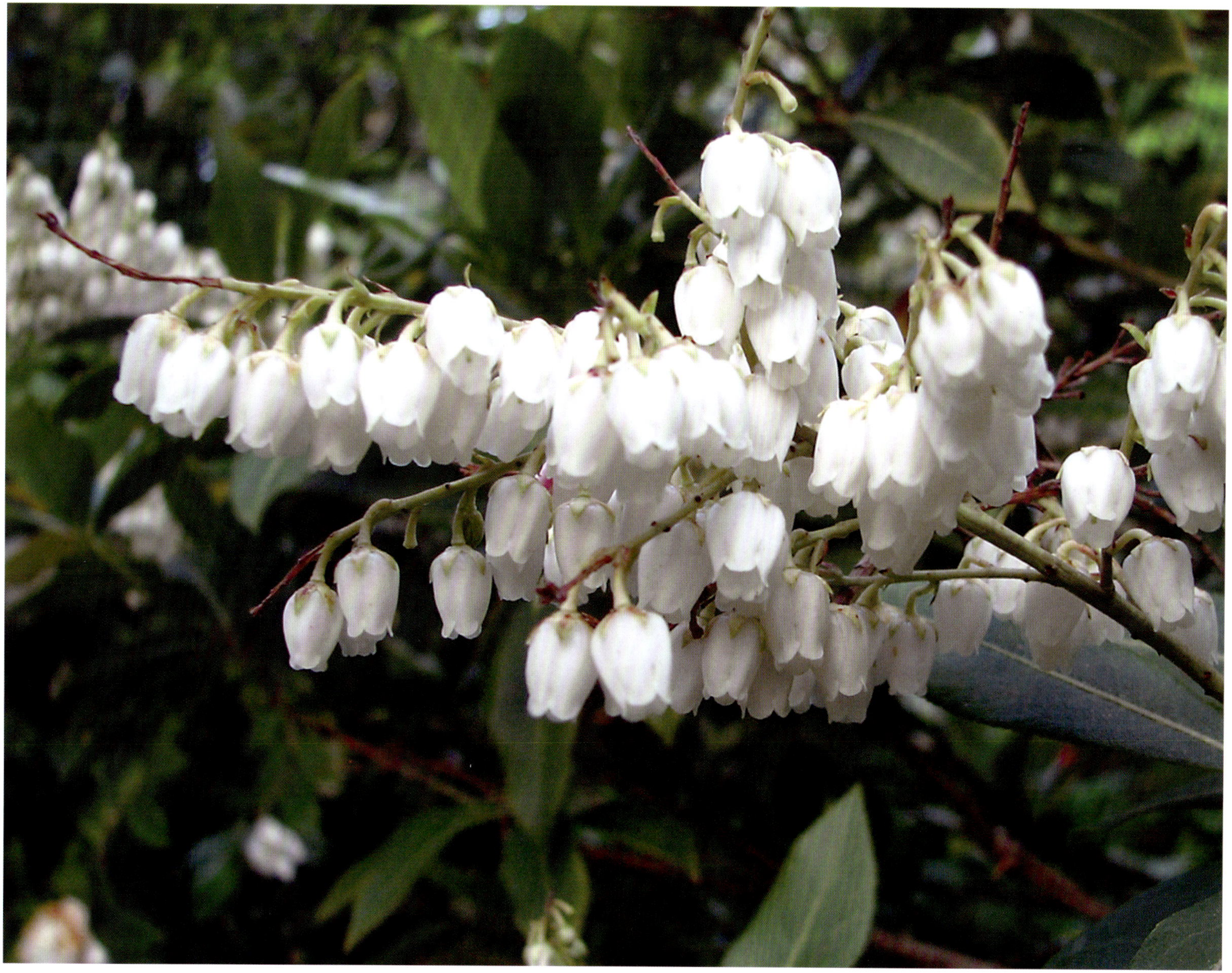

Rhododendrons can be had from low-growing shrubs to tree-size plants. They need shade, acid soil and a rainfall of 500 mm or more per annum for their best development. They enjoy cool-to-cold growing conditions but not long periods with little water.

Roses are for every garden because it is the only shrub that flowers for eight months of the year. Interplant them with other shrubs or grow them as a background to perennials such as Inca lilies or as a foreground to trees or climbers on fence or wall. Make holes 60 cm square and 45 cm deep if the ground is good and, if it is poor or sandy, make them larger. In the bottom put in old stable manure or a good compost mixed with some of the soil removed from the hole to within about 20 cm of ground level, and then plant the rose with its roots spread out around the hole. The union of the wild understock – that is, the section with roots – and the rose proper should be about level with or just below soil level, after planting. They prefer a cool-to-cold climate and do not flourish in subtropical gardens.

ABOVE: *Roses produce their lovely flowers in abundance in mid-spring and continue flowering until winter.* OPPOSITE: *Low-growing roses, like the one known as My Granny, are ideal for growing in large pots.*

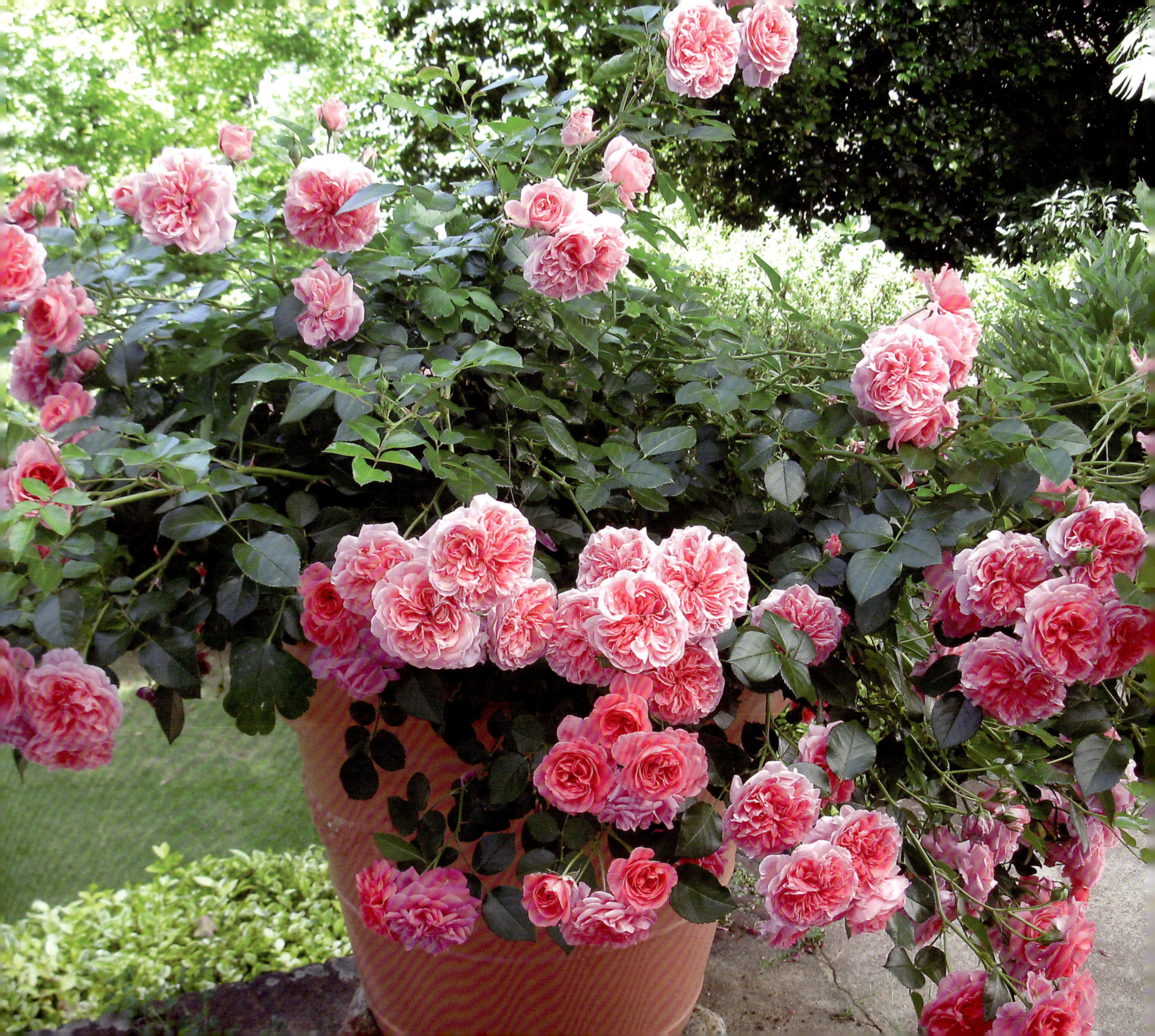

Snowball is one of the most rewarding of shrubs for the large garden. It stands both frost and fairly long periods of dryness when established. In spring it carries its decorative flowers and in early winter has brilliantly coloured leaves.

Syringa. Because this lovely tree seeds itself freely in parts of the summer-rainfall area it is on the list of trees which we may no longer grow. Such a pity as it is a good tree for regions with sharp frosts and a low rainfall, which cover a great deal of South Africa. The trees on this property are 60 years old and have never seeded themselves.

Valerian is one of the perennial plants I sowed about 60 years ago and it has appeared ever since to embellish in spring a dreary, unwatered bank, where it seeds itself and makes a delightful show for weeks.

The earliest of the climbers to flower in spring is wisteria. It is only too willing to grow and needs to be kept within bounds by an annual trimming immediately after flowering. Trimmed later, it may produce few or no flowers the following spring. It is both frost-hardy and drought-resistant. Its scented cascades of flowers appear before the leaves.

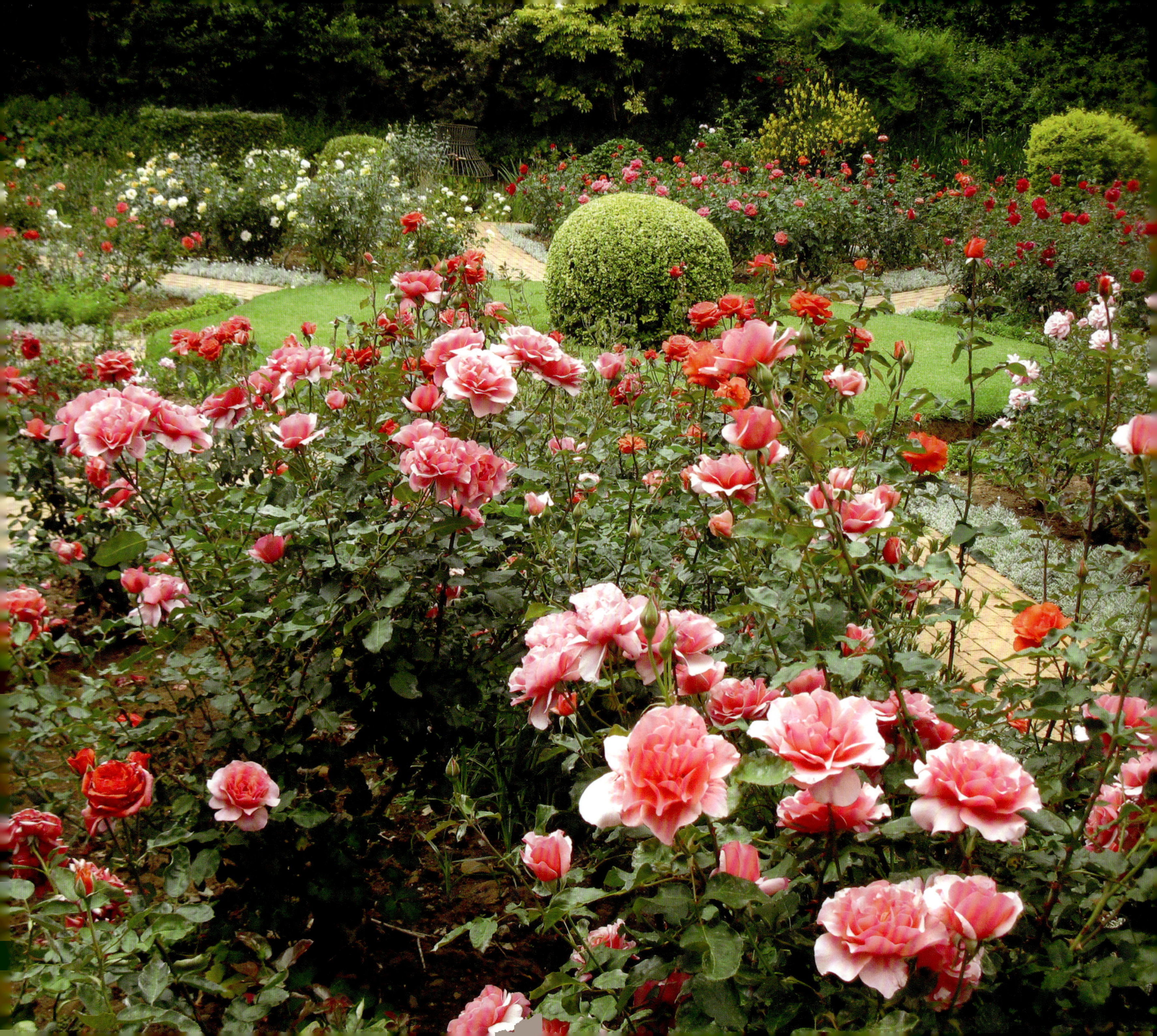

PART 11

SUMMER

Summer is the busiest time of the year because little rain falls between the beginning of November and mid-March. At this season we also experience days of intensely hot weather, and at the same time strong, drying wind is common.

From December to March the jet-watering systems operate day and night in order to cover the different areas of the garden twice a week. There is not enough water for the lawns and they have to rely on the occasional rain that may fall – a short downpour in the first two weeks of January and another in the last two weeks of February. The next one is usually mid-March.

All the lawns are of kikuyu grass. This is a robust grower and it will not die if it is not watered for three or four months, but of course it loses its verdant colour and by February it has a yellow tinge. Kikuyu has the reputation of spreading beyond its assigned limits, but this is compensated for by its willingness to grow under difficult conditions.

The jacaranda is the focal point in early summer when it casts its enchanting mauve mantle across the bench in the pergola. Here it flowers six to eight weeks later than it does upcountry and is at its best during December and up to Christmas. The flowers are a wonderful contrast in colour to the rich burgundy of the leaves of the copper beech and the golden robinia that grow nearby. What a pity a ban has been imposed country-wide on the planting of this beautiful tree. Mine, planted 65 years ago, has never produced a seedling.

Adding colour to the scene during the first month of summer are agapanthus, blue and white. The white are more vigorous in growth with larger flower heads and highlight the large, shady areas of the garden better than the blue. The areas between the terraces are steep slopes that are never watered, and that is where I planted them. When they are not in flower their neat leaves decorate the ground and keep it verdant. Towards the end of December, as the flowers of the agapanthus begin to go off, the shasta daisies take over.

A colourful shrub that flowers for a long time, starting in the first month of summer, is the yellow lantana. It is a tough plant which needs trimming back after its flowering is over. Some of our lovely wild crinums have their enchanting flowers at this time of the year and so do our yellow and pink arum lilies. Fifty years ago I brought back rootstock of the yellow arum from a farm in one of the coldest areas of the country. They did not multiply in my garden but they did produce their admirable flowers for the next ten years and then disappeared. I could

OPPOSITE: *The highlight of my garden over the Christmas period is the roses. If one cuts off the fading flowers in early-to-mid November, one will have a mass of blooms over the Christmas–New Year period. This is an important time in my life, for my children, grandchildren and great-grandchildren come from their homes around the globe – Australia, the United States and England – to celebrate Christmas in their ancestral homeland. I count myself very blessed indeed to have them all near at this time of the year. And, of course, it is a great joy to have the 11 youngest ones aged between 4 and 12 years playing happily together in the garden.*

In the Western Cape hydrangeas can be seen in small neglected gardens in roadside villages bearing masses of flowers on desiccated plants. In this garden where they are watered well and regularly, they grow into plants 1.5 m tall and are not as generous in their flowering. They're unpredictable but wonderful for colour in summer. They grow in frosty areas but do best near the coast.

not determine whether they had been dug up by an untrained gardener or whether an extremely wet winter had led to their demise.

Various climbers come into flower at the end of spring and continue into summer. Star jasmine is a delight because of the alluring scent of its tiny, starry white flowers. I have one with plain green leaves and another with variegated leaves. The former produces far more flowers than the latter. If not trained up a support, the species with green leaves will make an effective glossy carpet as it roots itself across the ground. Because of its robust growth it needs space to develop. Mandevilla is another climber with scented flowers at this time. The waxy white flowers consist of a tube ending in five segments. The rather sparse stems will twine around a trellis or the branches of a tree.

The different climbers that used to be listed as bignonias also bear their flowers in early summer. Most of them like warm growing conditions but will put up with fairly severe frost. The one once known as *Bignonia cherere* is now listed as *Distictis buccinatoria*. It is unfortunate that many of the botanical names of plants are so long and so difficult to pronounce and to remember. Fortunately there is usually a common name, and this exuberant and showy climber is known generally as the Mexican blood trumpet, or red trumpet climber. It needs space to develop its spreading stems. The Chinese trumpet climber (*Campsis grandiflora*) also flowers in mid-summer. It too is a vigorous plant suitable only for large gardens. It carries its apricot-coloured, trumpet-shaped flowers in large showy clusters.

Guinea gold vine is the name of an Australian climber with bright canary-yellow flowers with five rounded petals like those of a single rose. It has the additional merit of having densely arranged, lustrous leaves so that, if planted with the support of a fence or wall, it will form a pleasing screen. Bower vine is also native to Australia. This enthusiastic climber I have at the kitchen door. Its pretty, glossy, dark-green leaves are a fine foil to the clusters of funnel-shaped flowers that are white, flushed with deep pink in the throat.

The highlight of my garden over the Christmas period is the roses. If one cuts off the fading flowers in early-to-mid November, one will have a mass of blooms over the Christmas–New Year period. This is an important time in my life, for my children, grandchildren and great-grandchildren come from their homes around the globe – Australia, the United States and England – to celebrate Christmas in their ancestral homeland. I count myself very blessed indeed to have them all near at this time of the year. And, of course, it is a great joy to have the 11 youngest ones aged between 4 and 12 years playing happily together in the garden.

By Christmas some of the hydrangeas are in flower. These are wonderful plants for a show in summer whether in the garden or in pots. They like shade and tend to wilt if subjected to sunshine, except at the coast where they perform well in sun or shade. In acid soil they generally produce blue flowers and in alkaline soil the flowers will be pink.

Justicia, a shrub from Brazil with heads of coral-pink flowers, flaunts its beauty early in the New Year. It will grow in sun but does far better in shade. It has the advantage of having pretty leaves, so even when not in flower it makes a pleasing background. The impatiens and begonias continue to brighten various parts of the garden almost all through the summer. Dahlias, which were widely grown 30 years ago, make a splendid show in summer, and, as they are so easy to grow, I wonder why they are no longer popular. There are several different types, some of which are eminently suitable for small gardens.

By mid-January our native plant, the pineapple flower, dominates the area where it grows. Unfortunately its handsome spikes of flowers tend to lean over awkwardly if not staked. When it flowers the hydrangeas are beginning to change colour, and the two together make a dramatic show in a large arrangement. Both last for two to four weeks when picked. I am surprised that florists do not offer these two for sale in mid- to-late summer. Hibiscus enjoy the hot months of the year but, because of the shade, they do not produce an abundance of flowers here. For the same reason bougainvillaeas do not flower well. Moonflowers also produce their flowers of white, pink or ochre during the warm months. They do best where winters are mild. Two plants I would dearly like to have in the garden are frangipani and the climber known as beaumontia, but my garden is too cold. Both have pretty scented flowers.

Malvaviscus is a reliable summer-flowering shrub for a large garden.

I planted a group of Iceberg roses in a corner of the garden between the rose garden and the pergola about 15 years ago. They grew well and paraded their chaste snow-white flowers for all the world to admire for ten years, and then there emerged, rather shyly, from one of them, a stem bearing scarlet roses as well as white ones.

I like it because of its long flowering period and its readiness to grow in poor soil and without water. It flourishes where the drive leaves the main road and its pretty leaves make a verdant bower at the entrance. I have it growing near the house too because its soft-textured leaves look cool and lush on the hottest and driest of days. Its flowers of rich scarlet are cute but not showy. This is a plant to grow in a new garden between the newly planted trees, shrubs and climbers, to cover the bare ground until such permanent plants are large enough to make their presence felt. It needs to be cut back regularly as it grows fast, and, in a small garden, it should be removed as soon as the permanent plants are large enough to fill in the space.

During the last half of January and the parched days of February and March the garden is enlivened by the flowers of plumbago. I know of no other shrub that flowers for such a long period. This native plant will grow and flower even though never watered. The leaves are delicate in form and colour and the flowers are of a charming shade of blue. There is a species with white flowers but they look rather anaemic. The indigenous honeysuckle also does well under dry conditions. I interplanted yellow honeysuckle with plumbago along the main road some 50 years ago and have had the pleasure of their yellow and blue flowers ever since. Another indigenous shrub that makes a great show in summer is pride-of-de-Kaap. It has flowers of a rich apricot shade. As a foreground I planted the small-flowering blue agapanthus which comes into flower when the species with large flowers is over. These three shrubs are suitable only for medium-to-large gardens.

The main colour near the house during the hottest period of summer is provided by the leaves of shrubs and trees. This is when I most appreciate the rich colours of the copper beech, the prunus, the maples, the berberis and cannas, with the contrasting gold of golden abelia and privet, golden conifers and golden robinia and the variegated maples, plus the silver leaves of gazanias and dusty miller. Their leaves shine out boldly when there is little colour from flowers.

Towards the end of summer the weird flowers of the climber, aristolochia, make their appearance. I planted it in the pergola about 60 years ago, when I had no idea what it looked like as I had never seen a plant or even a picture of one. It developed slowly, with pleasing heart-shaped leaves, and in due course its huge flowers appeared, measuring 30 cm in length and 20 cm across. They are quite startling in size, shape and colour. Nearby, a cheerful combretum adds colour to the pergola. It has pretty glossy leaves which make a fine background to the spiky arrangement of flowers that are variously coloured through shades of gold, apricot and luminous bronze. It bears its flowers for at least five weeks. Next to it is a pride of India, which flaunts its showy flowers in late summer too. This small tree has heads of flowers that appear to be fashioned from crinkly paper, coloured pale to deep mauve, pale to deep pink, or white. It makes a splendid show for a long time during the hottest days of summer. We trim back the tree each winter to keep it within its allotted space in the garden. This also promotes better flowering.

The rose garden, which was full of flowers at Christmas time, has few flowers in February. From when the roses start their flowering in October we cut off the fading flowers every day until January. Because of the lack of rain in summer we want the plants to retain as many leaves as possible to help with the production of food and also to shade the ground. We do not want them to flower until the cool weather of autumn. In mid-to-late February we give the plants a very light trimming by cutting out weak-looking growth and shortening very long stems, by as much as we would when picking roses for arrangements. This ensures a wonderful show in autumn.

The last tree to come into flower at the end of summer is the Australian firewheel tree that I planted 50 years ago. It took 17 years to produce its first flowers. The scarlet flowers are unique in form. They resemble a wheel with many spokes. It is suitable only for a large garden where frosts are never more than mild. The last climber to flower in my garden in summer is a clematis from New Zealand, known as *Clematis paniculata*. This exuberant plant produces tens of thousands of tiny white, four-petalled flowers – forming a giant bridal garland spread along the pergola where it grows. The flowers have the scent of biscuits newly baked in honey and the bees love them. It makes a wonderful show for a month and is then trimmed back in order to keep it from spreading too far.

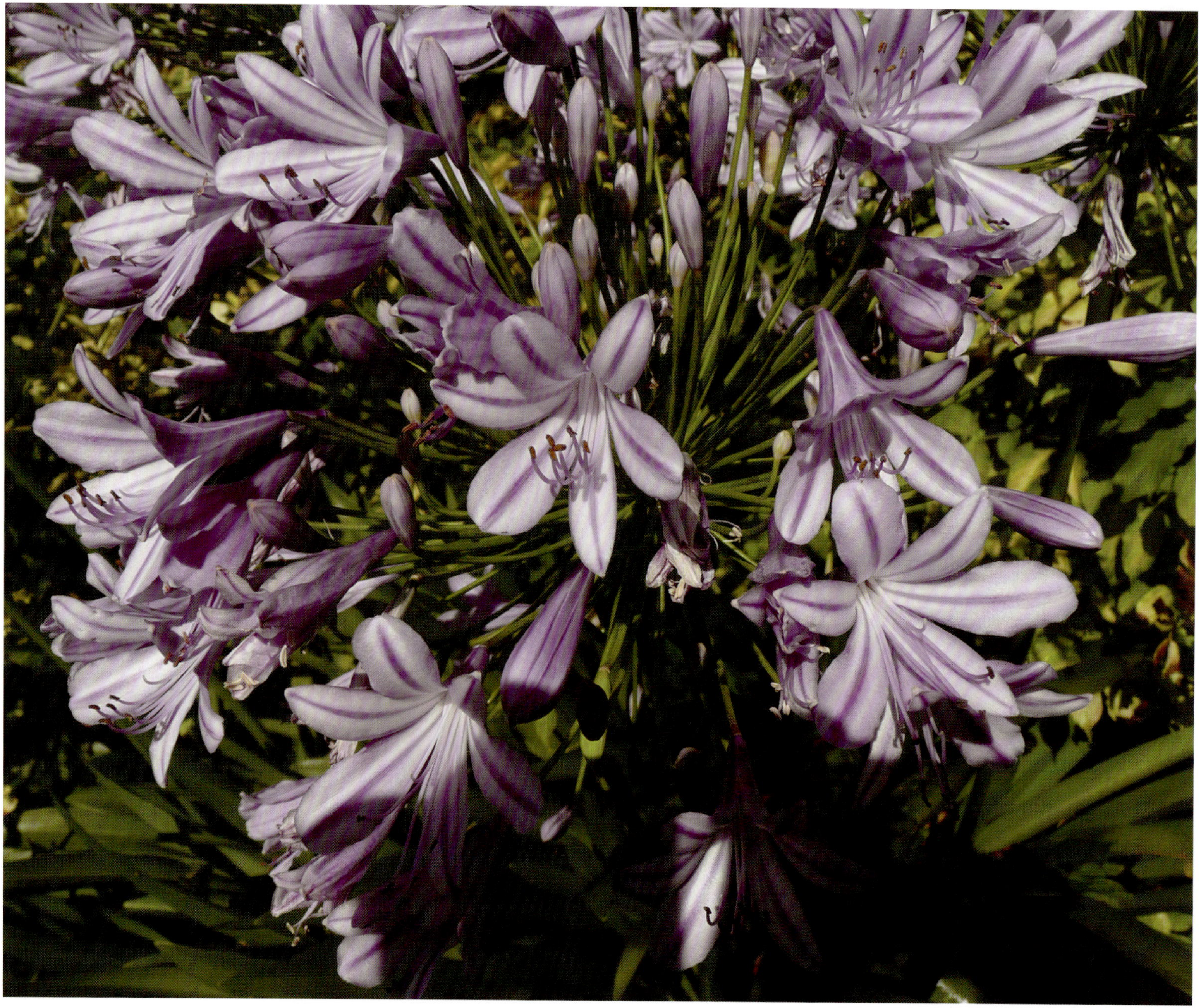

RIGHT: *This strange-looking flower commands attention rather than admiration! This species,* Aristolochia littoralis, *native to Brazil, is an evergreen plant with pretty heart-shaped leaves. It does not do well where winters are severe and needs regular watering.*

BELOW: *Australian myrtle (Australian brush cherry, Australian lilly pilly) has been used through generations as a hedge, but if left unclipped it develops into a pleasing, small evergreen tree six metres or more in height, with glossy leaves and pretty heads of flowers, which are followed by colourful fruits. It is tender to severe frost and should be watered regularly to promote quick growth. It is a good plant for coastal gardens.*

OPPOSITE: *Agapanthus is one of our native plants which are found growing in many gardens abroad. Here we planted it in a number of places where there is no watering system, along the drive and on steep banks. Its good-looking leaves cover the bare earth and its handsome flowers brighten the summer scene. It stands considerable frost and does well in gardens near the coast.*

Begonias are quick-growing perennials to use in shady areas. They should be planted in humus-rich soil. They need regular watering and are not frost-hardy.

Bower vine is a fast-growing evergreen climber with graceful stems of attractive, shining, dark-green leaves, composed of five to nine oval pointed leaflets. The flowers which festoon the plant in summer are coloured white or pale pink flushed with carnelian red in the throat. It does best where winters are mild. There is a related vigorous climber, wonga wonga vine, which occurs naturally in Australia, but it is not available locally.

Chinese trumpet climber is one of the decorative bignonia family. Its leaves are ornamental for most of the year and the large heads of apricot flowers add sparkle to the garden in mid-summer. It is hardy to severe frost but should be watered well in its first three or four years to establish a deep root system.

ABOVE: *Cotoneaster gladdens the mid-summer scene with its flowers arranged in decorative clusters. It is colourful too in autumn when the flowers become crimson berries. Hardy to frost and drought, it can be grown to tree form or else planted as a hedge where winters are severe.*

LEFT: *The flowers of this combretum are unique in form and attractive in colouring. Although it has long slender stems it can be trimmed to bush shape. The evergreen, pretty glossy leaves make a fine foil to its summer flowers and to the ornamental seeds that appear in autumn. It stands moderate frost.*

ABOVE: *Crinum.* This robust native plant is to be found growing wild in the summer-rainfall regions. It has a large bulb, long strap-shaped leaves and clusters of large lily-like flowers on sturdy erect stems. The plants should be watered during spring and summer. There are several species. This one is Crinum macowanii.

LEFT: *Crabapple fruits carried in decorative clusters festoon the trees in summer. This is a hardy deciduous tree of moderate size.*

Firewheel tree is an Australian one that needs space for its development as it may reach a height of 12 m. The large glossy leaves show up its unique coral-red flowers in clusters which make a brilliant show in late summer. It does best where winters are mild and the rainfall high.

Guinea gold vine (hibbertia). This Australian climber has decorative leaves 7 cm long, which look attractive throughout the year and make a splendid foil to the bright golden-yellow flowers that ornament the plant in late spring and summer. This is a half-hardy plant which stands moderate winters provided it gets enough water.

Hibiscus have been grown in our gardens for generations, and during the years many hybrids with single and double flowers of a wide range of shades have become available at our nurseries. I like the old, single-flower form with the throat of a darker shade than the outer part of the petals. It thrives in coastal and warm inland gardens.

ABOVE: *One of the most colourful of low-growing perennial plants for a show in summer is impatiens. They need shade and regular watering during their flowering period. They will survive moderate frost.*

LEFT: *Jacaranda is one of the most beautiful of the South American trees. Its grows much better in the summer rainfall area than in the region which has rain in winter. Although tender to frost when young it tolerates considerable frost and dryness after a few years growth. To encourage fast initial development water the young plant well through its first four years. Its height and spread is 10-12 metres. This is a shallow-rooted tree and shrubs and other plants growing near it may suffer.*

Justicia produces its pretty flowers in mid-summer. The plant is a quick-growing Brazilian one, reaching a metre or more in height and spread, and enlivens the garden for weeks with its coral-pink flowers. It likes dappled shade and does not thrive in frosty gardens. Trim back the plants after their flowering is over to about 80 cm.

ABOVE LEFT: *Lantana is another native of Central South America that thrives under difficult conditions. The form here illustrated does well in poor soil and tolerates long dry periods and fairly severe frost when well established. The plant should be lightly pruned each year to keep it from becoming straggly and to promote better flowering.*

ABOVE RIGHT: *Malvaviscus is a large shrub that grows fast to a height of two to three metres and has a wide spread. Its velvety vine-shaped leaves, unevenly notched at the edges, have a luxurious appearance. Although not watered for the four dry months from late spring to the end of summer, its leaves keep their fresh appearance. The pretty little flowers show up well against the dark leaves. This shrub is not recommended for frosty gardens.*

OPPOSITE: *Mauve bignonia is a decorative evergreen climber from the Argentine which starts flowering in late spring and continues in summer, producing delightful lilac trumpet flowers in clusters which show up attractively against its dark-green leaves. When well grown, it will endure sharp frost and fairly dry conditions.*

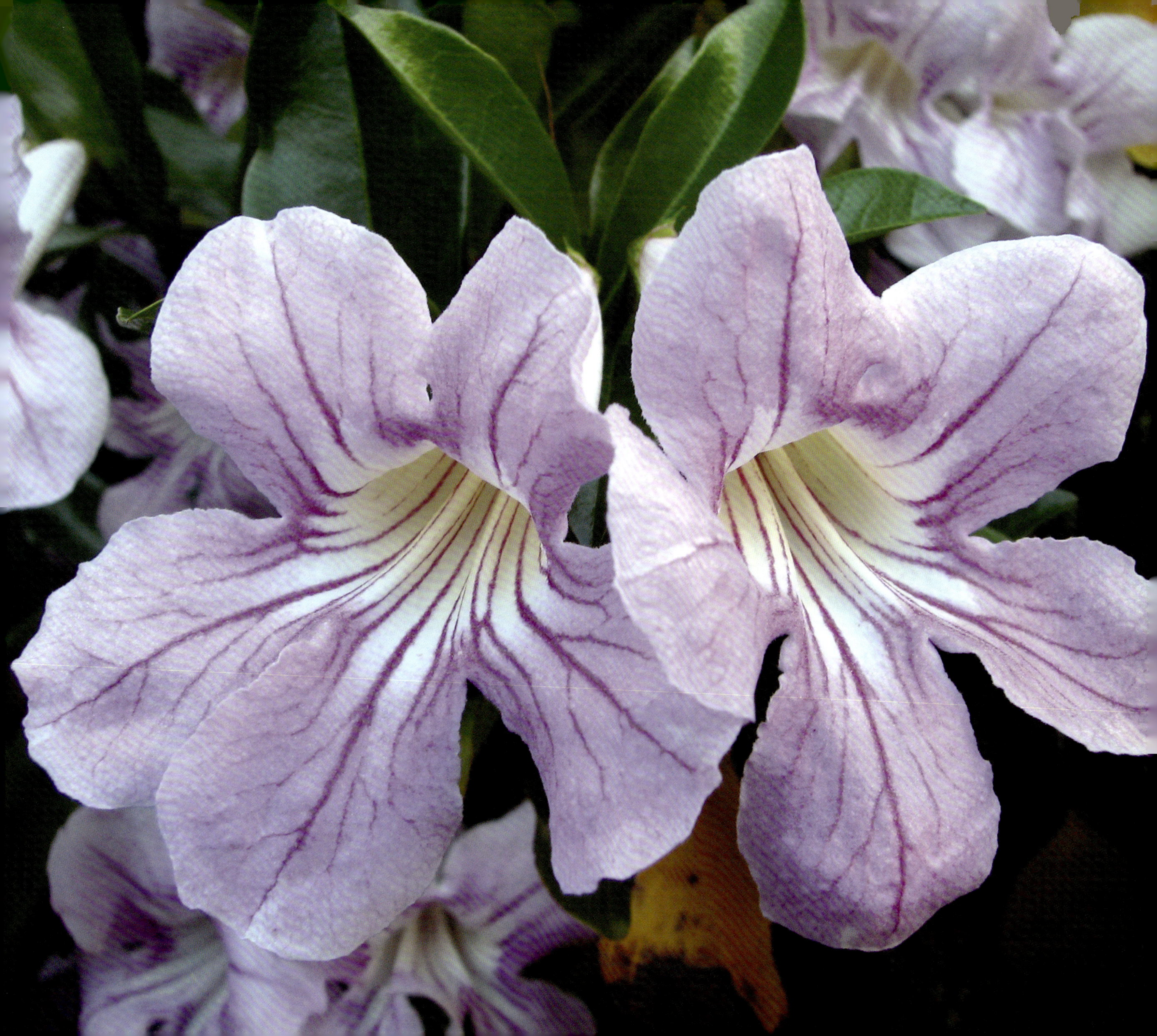

ABOVE: Mexican blood trumpet has been re-named botanically three times since I first grew it. This plant may still be known to some as Bignonia cherere.
It is one of the most vigorous of climbers, producing an abundance of its large, richly coloured flowers in flamboyant clusters in late spring and summer. It tolerates fairly sharp frost and, once established, will grow through long periods with little water. Trim it back hard when flowering is over or it may cover the house!

ABOVE LEFT: Moonflowers are quick-growing small trees native to South America. The seeds are hallucenogenic and all parts of the plant are poisonous. My three plants, about 20 years old, have not affected my grandchildren or great-grand-children and their friends, so I leave them to grow and produce their large, showy flowers. They do best in warm gardens but will tolerate some frost. The large white one is known as Brugmansia x candida.

LEFT: Brugmansia sanguinea has flowers of a different shape, coloured pale to dark orange.

ABOVE: *Paulownia, a beautiful deciduous tree native to China, will reach a height and spread of about ten metres. The ornamental, large, heart-shaped leaves are soft in texture and mid-green in colour. It produces glorious clusters of mauve flowers rather like those of a foxglove in shape. Paulownia does best in regions with cool, wet winters. It stands considerable frost but not dry conditions.*

RIGHT: *The lovely ethereal white moonflower flushed with palest pink is* Brugmansia x insignis.

New Zealand clematis is a fast-growing evergreen climber with pretty leaves and garlands of small scented flowers. This species does best in gardens where winters are mild but will also grow in frosty areas where it should be planted so that it is shaded from the early morning sun.

Pineapple flower has been aptly named as the top of the flower-spike does indeed resemble the top of a pineapple. It is a handsome flower that lasts for up to three weeks in an arrangement. Unfortunately, to look its best in the garden it needs to be tied to a stake to keep it erect. It grows wild in the summer-rainfall regions. The plant thrives in full sun or dappled shade and is tolerant of cold winters.

LEFT: *Plumbago is one of the most adaptable of our indigenous shrubs. It tolerates months with no water. This close-up picture emphasises the beauty of each cluster of flowers.*

BELOW: *There are few trees that flower in summer and I therefore value pride of India for its determination to bring lustre to the garden during the brittle dry days of late summer. It takes kindly to an annual trimming and is a good tree for gardens large and small. It has the additional merit of enhancing the garden again in winter when the leaves turn from amber to russet to burnished bronze. Unfortunately, under humid conditions the plant is affected by mildew.*

OPPOSITE: *A summer scene from the front garden looking across towards the rose garden. In the foreground is the rose Pinkie, backed by the silver leaves of lamb's ear. The shrub with bronze leaves is Berberis thunbergii 'Rose Glow'. In front and behind it are golden privets and, in the background, the colourful American maple (Acer negundo 'Variegatum'). The small shrub next to it is a golden duranta and, higher up the slope, is a golden elder. At the top of the slope is a burgundy prunus (Prunus cerasifera 'Nigra'). Left, foreground, is a trimmed golden abelia.*

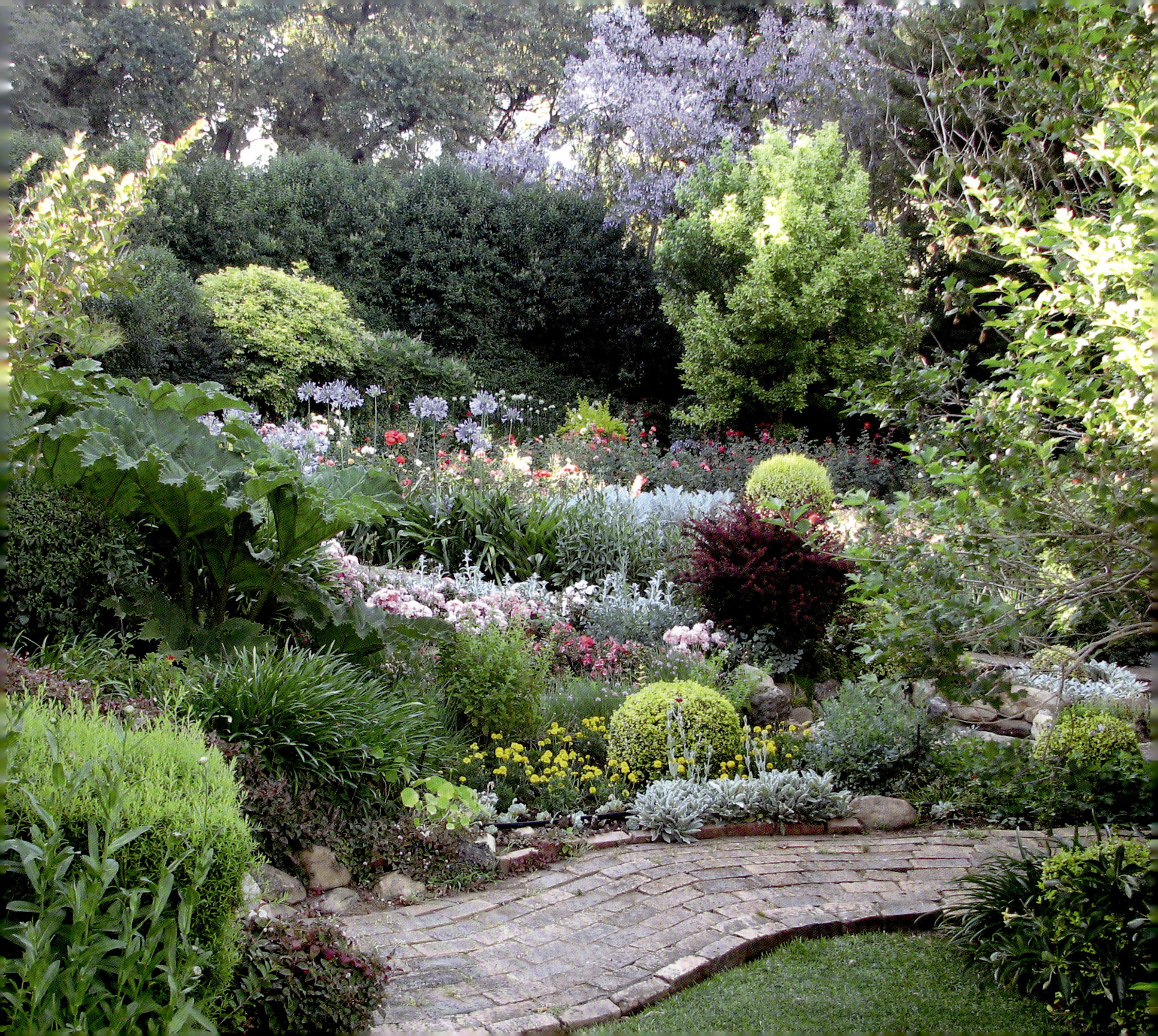

ABOVE: *Sky flower is an exuberant climber which needs to be trimmed back after its flowering period is over. It does best in gardens where winters are mild and when watered regularly. Because of its rampant growth it is recommended only for the medium-to-large garden.*

ABOVE LEFT: *Shasta daisies are sun-loving plants that start their flowering when the agapanthus are almost past their prime, and therefore enhance the garden when there is little else in flower. In a shady garden, such as this one, white flowers serve to brighten the scene. Shasta daisies grow and multiply quickly, and in a small garden need annual attention to prevent them taking over too much space.*

LEFT: *Yellow trumpet climber is one of many beautiful plants native to Brazil. Its neat, glossy, leathery leaves are attractive throughout the year, and in late spring and early summer it produces its showy clusters of daffodil-yellow trumpet flowers. It does not do well where frosts are severe.*

OPPOSITE: *Water lilies are deciduous summer-flowering water plants grown for their decorative floating leaves and their highly ornamental flowers. They do best in full sun and still water. The plants grow from tuber-like rhizomes and should be lifted and divided in winter every three or four years. The flowers are from ivory through many shades of pink to rose and yellow.*

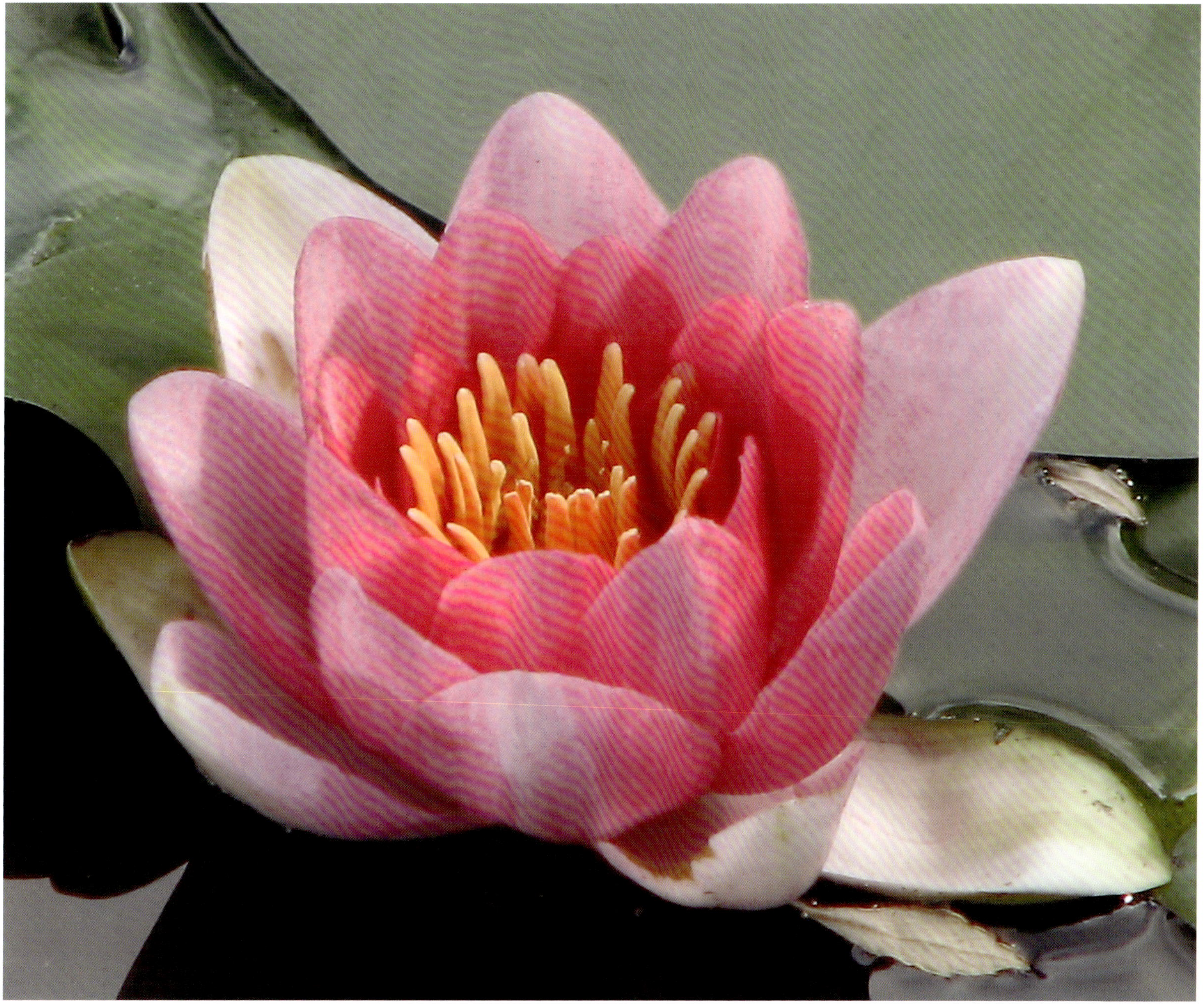

In this scene the golden glow of an autumn sunset highlights every plant, creating a lovely luminous picture.

PART 11

AUTUMN

There is a harmony
In Autumn, and a lustre in the sky,
Which thro' the summer is not heard nor seen,
As it could not be, as if it had not been
– Shelley

I am delighted when autumn comes and we can say a joyous farewell to the dreary south-east winds that blow each week during the summer months, sometimes non-stop for three days. As the days shorten and become cooler and the rains begin to fall regularly, we can spend more time on general maintenance than on watering, which demands a great deal of time and effort all through summer.

In March several indigenous plants bring colour to the scene and all of them are easy to grow. Plumbago, our native honeysuckle and the belladonna lily, which starts flowering in February, continue to highlight their areas during March and, later in the month, plectranthus and crocosmia add colour to shady areas and bulbine and crassula to the sunny spots. Of the shrubs, spur flower (plectranthus) dominates the scene. There are more than 40 plectranthus species to be found growing wild in South Africa and, as many of them are excellent garden subjects, it is surprising that so few nurseries propagate them. The plants vary in size from prostrate-growing ones which look attractive in pots or hanging baskets or as ground covers, to shrubs a metre or more in size. They do best in shade and they are tolerant of drought and moderate frost. The colours of the flowers are from white to blush pink and mauve to a royal blue. I have several of them. The one known as *Plectranthus ecklonii* produces its delightful conical heads of tiny blue flowers on rounded shrubs more than a metre high and wide. Nearby is another with a frothy mass of pink and white flowers. The low-growing ones embellish pots on a terrace in another part of the garden. Because of the speed and vigour of their growth they need to be reduced in size after their flowering period.

The flowers of the belladonna lily come as a surprise late in February or early in March. The name means 'beautiful lady' – a very apt one as its large flowers are spectacular. With most plants one is aware that a bud is developing, but in the case of this indigenous plant the flowering stem noses its way out from ground that is bare, as the plant loses its leaves before it sends up a flowering stem. Within two days of the emergence of the shoot, the stem has grown to 45–60 cm and has a cluster of ethereal, ivory-flushed pink flowers at its tip. It is one of my favourites as it shows off its beauty no matter how neglected. In nature one finds it growing in shade or in full sun, at the seaside and on dry banks. It is a most adaptable plant. More than 30 years ago whilst travelling in New Zealand I visited a nurseryman, then in his 80s. He loved hybridising plants and had crossed our pink arum with the yellow one and produced a large yellow

The Sansanqua camellias are amongst the most decorative of large shrubs or small trees for autumn colour. They can be grown successfully in large pots. For their specific needs, consult the notes in the chapter on Winter.

arum with a pink edge. He had also produced a deep-pink belladonna lily. He photographed it, posted the pictures to a large firm of bulb growers in Holland, and, a week before I visited him, he had received a cable from them ordering 10,000 bulbs at a dollar each. Alas, he had only 100 and it would be at least another three to five years before he would have that number to send.

I often wonder why we South Africans, who are blessed with such a wealth of wild flowers, have done so little to promote their development commercially. The New Zealanders were growing our proteaceae for export to the cut-flower trade 40 years ago and they have created hybrids from many of our native plants.

I cannot remember when I planted the corms of crocosmia but they have multiplied and spread to different shady areas. There are several species. I have *Crocosmia aurea*, which grows to 60 cm in height and has long, slender, tapering leaves that come out like a fan on each side of the stalk. The flame-coloured flowers carried in spikes shine out cheerfully in the shadowy patches they colonise. Corms planted in August will flower the following March. They are hardy to fairly severe frost.

The lovely red nerine, *Nerine sarniensis*, which created a sensation in Europe when it was first grown there, also flowers now. This plant was an early traveller, for it is recorded that in 1634 one species flowered in a garden in Paris, and it was cultivated in England by 1659. The story of how a species from the Cape came to be called the Guernsey lily is an interesting one. In 1659, a Dutch ship proceeding from the Far East via the Cape to Holland was wrecked on the Channel Islands, and boxes of Cape bulbs consigned to Holland were washed ashore on the island of Guernsey. There they grew and produced their lovely scarlet flowers. The plants multiplied and flourished on the island and in due course became one of the finest flowers grown on the islands for export to florists in Europe. Because it grew so well, and had grown there for so many years, it was named *Nerine sarniensis*, the word Sarnia being the old name for the island. At one time it was thought to be a native of Japan, since the vessel which was wrecked was on its way from the Orient. It was only a century later, when specimens were found growing on the slopes of Cape Town's Table Mountain, that its real origin became known. This species, and hybrids developed from it, are widely grown in England, the United States, Australia and New Zealand as pot plants, as well as in the garden, and to provide cut flowers in autumn.

The red crassula, *Crassula falcata*, has scarlet flowers carried in flat heads about 15 cm across, on stems 45–60 cm high. *Crassula multicava* is a useful ground cover for dry banks that get little or no water. It romps along in sun or shade, covering the ground with its fleshy leaves, and produces a frothy mass of tiny star-shaped flowers coloured ivory to blush-pink. All it needs is to be trimmed back from time to time to prevent it from invading the whole garden. Both species stand moderate frost.

Japanese anemone is an exuberant perennial I planted in the woodland garden many years ago because of its pretty leaves and poppy-like flowers that appear on slender stems 45-60 cm tall. The flowers are white or pink. I grow only the white as it shows up far better in dense shade. The plant tends to spread with reckless abandon. There are a number of decorative plants in my garden that spread rapidly either by seeding or by roots. Where they invade areas allotted to other plants we dig them up (good exercise) and where they appear in paths or other paved areas we apply weedkiller. We mix this in a bowl according to directions and, using an 8-cm-wide paint brush, we 'paint' the top leaves of the unwanted plants. This is a quicker and safer method than using a spray pump and there is no danger of the weedkiller getting on the leaves of other plants.

Towards the end of March the glossy bronze-to-cyclamen fruits of the Australian myrtle add a touch of colour near the fence along the road. This plant is usually grown as a hedge, but if it is not trimmed it will become a tree six metres high with densely arranged foliage. I planted three to hide the road from view and also to dampen the sound of the traffic.

By mid-April the leaves of the Lombardy poplars begin to fall as they slowly turn from green to gold. Whereas some trees lose all their leaves quickly, these poplars take their time to do so, and it is generally only

This combretum is another plant that flaunts its beauty twice a year. When the attractive flowers that appear in summer fade, they become russet to plum-coloured seed capsules that remain decorative for weeks.

in late May that they are entirely bare of leaves. The intensity of the fall colour depends on the weather, and in some years the colours are more vibrant than in others.

The most vibrant colour of all at this time of the year is that of the leaves of the persimmon. An astonishing combination of yellows, orange and russet flushes their glossy leaves for two to three weeks, and, as soon as it has lost its leaves, those of the wax tree flame into a rich ruby-red. It sheds its leaves quickly, but for three weeks the area where it grows commands attention. It is native to the warmer parts of China and Japan and, in days gone by, candles were made from the waxy fruit, which accounts for the common name.

Of the great and noble trees my favourite is the liquidambar. It has every attribute: a good shape, a handsome branch structure, beautifully shaped leaves of a pleasing light-green in summer and of dazzling shades of autumn colour for three to four weeks. Because of its height and spread it is, however, suitable only for large gardens and parks.

There are another two majestic and unique trees that I much admire when I look down on them as I walk along the pergola. They are now as tall as the Lombardy poplars – pushing 30–35 metres. They are native to China and have the cumbersome name of *Sequoia glyptostroboides*. As they have no common name and are related to the giant redwoods of California, the biggest trees in the world, I refer to them as the Chinese redwoods. Like the coelacanth, this tree was known only in fossil remains until 1945 when a grove of them was found in a remote area of China. In 1949 I was given two rooted cuttings by the late Dr Brian Rycroft, who was at one time Professor of Botany at the University of Cape Town and Director of Kirstenbosch Botanical Garden. Would that he could stand at their feet now and admire his gift. It certainly is much appreciated by me.

By the end of April many of the deciduous trees are showing a change of colour. The only evergreen trees that we have in flower at this time are the sasanqua camellias. They produce ethereal single flowers of snowy white, pale pink or rose with a rich centre of gold stamens that shine out against their pale petals. They continue to flower for two months until well after the Japanese camellias have started their flowering. If I had a very small garden (and if the situation, soil and climate were suitable) I would plant one each of these two different types of camellia, as the leaves are handsome throughout the year and the flowers are produced from early autumn all through winter until early spring. Add two other small trees for colour contrast – the golden robinia which loses its leaves in autumn, though for nine months of the year they make a splendid contrast to the deep-green leaves of the camellias, and a Japanese maple with burgundy leaves.

The rose garden in April is almost as colourful as in spring, as the trimming of the plants we do in late February and the moisture in the air that comes with the first autumn rains produce a surge of growth and flowering. The dampness of course also fosters the development of fungus diseases, so it brings its problems too. We have to spray to combat the afflictions known as black spot and rust.

Pyracantha and cotoneaster are two large shrubs that produce their colourful orange and red berries at this time. Pyracantha, which has strong, sharp thorns, is useful as an impenetrable hedge around a large property. They are both hardy to frost and drought and they can both be trimmed as they grow to form shade trees about three to four metres tall and four metres across.

A quick-growing native shrub that bears a profusion of flowers is the ribbon bush. Its velvety leaves are decorative through the year and its large conical heads of pale-mauve flowers almost hide the leaves in mid-autumn. Each little flower consists of a tube reflexed at the top and marked with paler mauve. It is a very useful plant to put in as a stop-gap whilst slow-growing ones develop.

In early April the chorisia loses its pretty leaves and then the flowers begin to open, and in early-to-mid May, when it is in full flower, it is a stunning sight. Mine is growing as a background tree beyond the garden and next to a Californian redwood. For the four to six weeks that it is in flower each day I have my morning tea on the north stoep where I can admire its handsome branch structure and colourful canopy, with camellias nearby filling in the foreground.

ABOVE: *Australian myrtle (eugenia, lilly pilly tree) has been a favourite hedging plant in our country for generations. Untrimmed, it will grow into a small tree. It takes kindly to pruning and therefore makes a good evergreen hedge for small as well as large gardens. The lustrous foliage is a fine background to its heads of fluffy summer flowers and its cherry-red fruits that appear in autumn and early winter. This is a frost-tender plant that does well in coastal gardens.*

ABOVE RIGHT: *The belladonna lily, sometimes known as the March lily, is native to the winter-rainfall region. The botanical name translates as 'beautiful lady' and well does it deserve this soubriquet. The flowers appear after the leaves have died down and their delicate loveliness is emphasised by the lack of leaves. They are to be found growing wild in the coastal bush in the sand and on dry gravel hill-slopes. They flower under extremely harsh conditions. It grows from a large bulb, which should be planted about 15 cm deep and spaced 30 cm apart. To ensure first-class flowers, add compost to the soil before planting.*

RIGHT: *Camellias for autumn flowers belong to the group known as* Camellia sasanqua. *Their flowers, single and semi-double, are of exceptional beauty.*

I came across this magnificent tree from Brazil by chance about 40 years ago. I was driving through the Cape Town suburb of Claremont when a tree with a glorious head of flowers showed up ahead, allowing me just enough time to move across the traffic into the garden where it was growing. The owners of the property did not know the name of the tree nor where I could procure a plant, but indicated that they thought the previous owners had obtained it from a nursery about 300 kilometres east of Johannesburg. I knew of an old, well-established nursery in that area that dealt mainly in fruit trees. I wrote to them – Hall's Nursery – and back came the answer that they could supply me with plants and gave me the name of the tree, its origin and the story of how they propagated the first plants in this country.

In 1951 Mrs Hall (wife of the founder of the nursery) returned from a visit to Brazil with a baby's pillow bought in that country. Feeling something hard inside the pillow she decided to investigate and, on opening it, discovered that the hard, pea-like lumps were seeds embedded in the kapok. The seeds were sown and gave rise to the first trees to be grown in a nursery in South Africa. This tree, *Chorisia speciosa*, sometimes referred to as the kapok tree, produces very large, hard seedpods about 18 cm long in which there is a mass of kapok surrounding the small seeds.

Towards the end of autumn the birches decide to take centre-stage. Their dancing top-leaves start the show with a flush of gold that is a wonderful contrast to their silver boles. Every evening, as the sun sets, I watch, for half an hour or so, as the sinking sun backlights the golden leaves and, as I watch, the leaves keep floating languorously to the ground.

Pride of India, whose flowers enhanced the garden during the hot dry days of February, brings colour to the scene again in late May and early June when its glossy leaves turn burnished crimson before they fall.

In late autumn, here and there in the garden, one comes across a cheerful climber commonly known as canary creeper because of the colour of its flowers. This quick-growing climber can be seen growing wild in the warmer regions of South Africa. The clusters of flowers are striking. Each little flower is like a tiny daisy, but the clusters are large, up to 16 cm across.

Another exuberant climber that makes a great show when its leaves change colour in late autumn and early winter is the Virginia creeper. This is a splendid plant to cover a wall or fences in a large garden. It has the merit of being self-supporting, clinging to a wall or fence by its sucker-like discs. I have it decorating the walls of the old dairy in the back garden. The leaves, deep green for much of the year, turn the most glorious, scintillating colours before dropping. This climber has to be trimmed back once a year – not a difficult task. It is hardy to drought as well as frost.

All year through I look forward to the flowering of the luculia in late autumn. This is a difficult plant to grow and to propagate. I planted three but only one has flowered well. It is protected from wind by the walls of the house. One died, I think, because of an excessively dry summer and insufficient water in the ground and moisture in the air. The other sulks because it is in too much shade. Luculia grows wild in the foothills of the Himalayas, where winters are mild and misty conditions prevail. It is a small tree that grows to about six metres in its native habitat. Mine, after ten years, is two metres tall and is a lanky bush, but the flowers are beautiful beyond imagining and their scent is beyond description. The tubular flowers of delicate shell-pink are carried in round clusters about 10–15 cm in diameter.

The combretum in the pergola, which had its decorative flowers in mid-summer, now draws attention to its attractive nut-brown seedpods that show up well against its pretty leaves. I like plants that produce decorative seeds or colourful leaves after having had pretty flowers in a previous season. At this time of the year the autumn colours of the flowers of the hydrangeas also make a delightful show in the many areas where they grow. These mature flowers last for a long time in arrangements. Their colours are a subtle green mixed with pale mauve, ochre and bronze – quite lovely in the garden and in arrangements. Hydrangeas can be pruned during autumn, but where winters are severe this should be delayed until late winter.

ABOVE: *Chorisia, a Brazilian tree, is a magnificent sight when in full flower. It has a good branch structure and pretty leaves and is therefore of ornamental value throughout the year. It loses its leaves in late summer or early autumn just before it flowers, so that the flowers stand out clearly against the bare stems and the sky. The bole of the tree is armed with strong thorns. Chorisia grows quickly in subtropical gardens where the rainfall is high. It stands moderate frost and, under ideal conditions, reaches a height of ten metres or more, with a spread of as much. It is therefore suitable only for the large garden or park.*

ABOVE LEFT: *The silver birch was introduced to our gardens only about 20 years ago. With its gleaming silver bole, its elegant branch structure and its delicate stems of golden leaves, it makes a particularly fine show in autumn but it is a decorative tree throughout the year. Though it is native to the coldest countries of Europe, it nevertheless endures our very hot, dry summers. Water well during its first three years to promote sturdy growth.*

LEFT: *Canary creeper is to be found growing wild in many parts of South Africa. It is a quick-growing, forest plant with light-green, slightly succulent leaves shaped somewhat like those of an ivy. It makes a pretty screen when trained against a fence or wall, or when growing up into a tree. The large clusters of canary-yellow, daisy-like flowers make a bright show. It is a very fast-growing plant and should be trimmed back in spring. It is not recommended for areas of severe frost but will tolerate fairly dry growing-conditions.*

Each individual flower of the chorisia is exquisitely formed and delicately coloured lilac with a flush of pale gold in the throat flecked with maroon.

ABOVE: *Crocosmia is to be found growing in woodlands in different regions of our country. The plants produce pretty sprays of dainty flowers poised like butterflies in shades of flame on stems 40–60 cm tall. They grow from cormous roots which should be planted in early spring near the surface of the soil and about 30 cm apart. They do best in dappled shade.*

ABOVE LEFT: *Cotoneaster (pronounced kuh-tone-ee-aster) is covered with clusters of small ivory flowers in summer. In autumn these become bright scarlet berries which remain on the plant for two to three months. It is thus of decorative value for a long time. Cotoneasters can be relied upon to grow under almost any conditions. They endure severe cold, survive long periods with little water and do fairly well in poor soil.*

LEFT: *Hawthorn is yet another summer-flowering plant that has clusters of small, ruby-red berries in autumn. It enjoys cold growing conditions and, once established, will endure long, dry periods too. The one growing in this garden is a deciduous tree rising to 6 metres in height and spread. The leaves turn red in spring and are followed by clusters of white flowers and later by red berries. It has long, strong thorns and is suitable for a large impenetrable hedge.*

ABOVE: *Our indigenous honeysuckle with bright orange flowers can be seen growing wild in coastal bush. The yellow form makes a finer show and blends better with most other colours than does the one with orange flowers. Its flowering period is longer than that of many other shrubs. They are rich in nectar, which attracts the butterflies and bees. This is a robust plant only too eager to grow, tolerant of mild frost and dry conditions. It does best in coastal regions. It can be tried in a small garden if it is cut back each year after its flowering is over. Untrimmed, it tends to become rather straggly in appearance.*

ABOVE RIGHT: *Hydrangeas ornament the garden through most of summer and for weeks in autumn when their drying flowers become papery and change to a variety of colours from jade-green through amber to shades of russet. They last very well indeed in dried arrangements.*

RIGHT: *The Japanese anemone is a fine perennial with flower stems rising to 60–80 cm in height. It seeds itself freely and has to be weeded out occasionally. This is a shade-loving plant with attractive leaves and poppy-like flowers with prominent stamens of pure gold. They highlight the deep pools of shade in the garden. It is hardy to frost and tolerant of fairly dry conditions.*

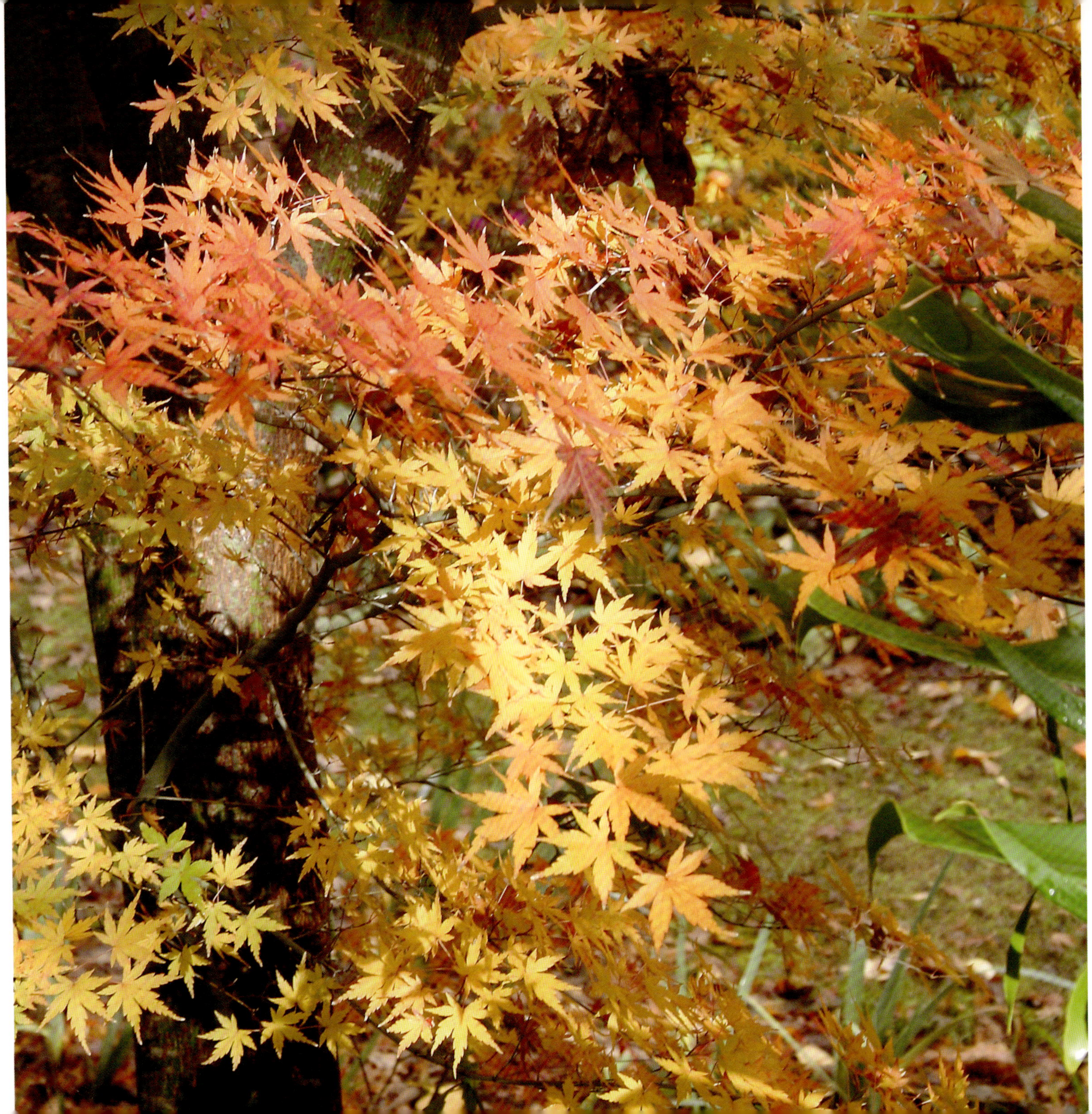

ABOVE: *Liquidambar is one of the grandest of trees we grow, but it is suitable only for very large gardens. It may reach a height of 25 m or more and have a basal spread of 15–20 m. Its leaves make a noble show for much of the year and particularly in autumn when they turn luminous flame colours. It enjoys cold frosty winters but is not for gardens where the rainfall is low.*

OPPOSITE: *The leaves of the Japanese maples begin to turn colour in autumn but are at their brightest in winter. This is a tree for gardens large and small. Cultural needs are given in the chapter on Winter.*

ABOVE: *Luculia has the most glorious of flowers with a wonderful fragrance on lanky bushes. The flowers of palest shell-pink are carried in rounded clusters about 15 cm in diameter. Luculia hails from the lower Himalayas and tolerates moderate frost but not long dry periods. It grows to three metres in height and spreads across about two metres. Water well to encourage good flowering.*

LEFT: *Lombardy poplar. This is a wonderful tree to plant as a focal point in a large garden or park. Its tall, slender silhouette commands attention throughout the year and in autumn the golden leaves are an arresting sight. When established, it stands extreme cold and long periods of dryness. Because of its root spread it should be planted ten or more metres from a building.*

The persimmon is not usually regarded as a plant for the home garden, but it can be included in a large garden because it is one of the first to change colour early in autumn and the colours are lovely, from amber to russet to ruby-red. It grows to six to nine metres with a spread of almost as much. After the leaves drop, large edible fruits of a lovely tomato-red adorn the tree. Once the tree is established it stands fairly severe frost and long periods of dry weather.

Spur flower or plectranthus. The botanical name includes shrubs and low-growing plants. The species here illustrated is a shrub that enlivens the autumn scene with large heads of flowers shaded from white through palest pink to purple. It grows wild in forests in different areas of the summer-rainfall region. This is a vigorous plant that reaches a height and spread of a metre within a year or two. Good for coastal gardens. Inland, they should be grown in dappled shade.

LEFT: *Plumbago is one of my favourite shrubs for practical reasons. It grows with no water; it thrives in poor soil; it stands quite severe frost; it takes kindly to hard trimming; and it produces charming heads of delightful sky-blue flowers for two to three months. I know of no other plant that flowers for as long and demands no attention other than trimming after flowering is over and, once in three to four years, the removal of excess roots that develop from the original roots.*

BELOW: *Pyracantha is a hardy shrub, tolerant of frost and drought. Too large for the small garden, it is ideal as a hedge plant for a large area as its numerous sharp thorns are a deterrent to intruders. It has flowers in summer and clusters of flame-coloured berries in autumn.*

OPPOSITE: *Ribbon bush is a quick-growing indigenous shrub to one to two metres, with soft, sage-green foliage and masses of dainty pale-mauve flowers in autumn. To keep it tidy, trim the plant back to 60 cm after its flowering is over. It is not hardy to frost but does well in coastal gardens. In hot dry gardens, plant it in partial shade.*

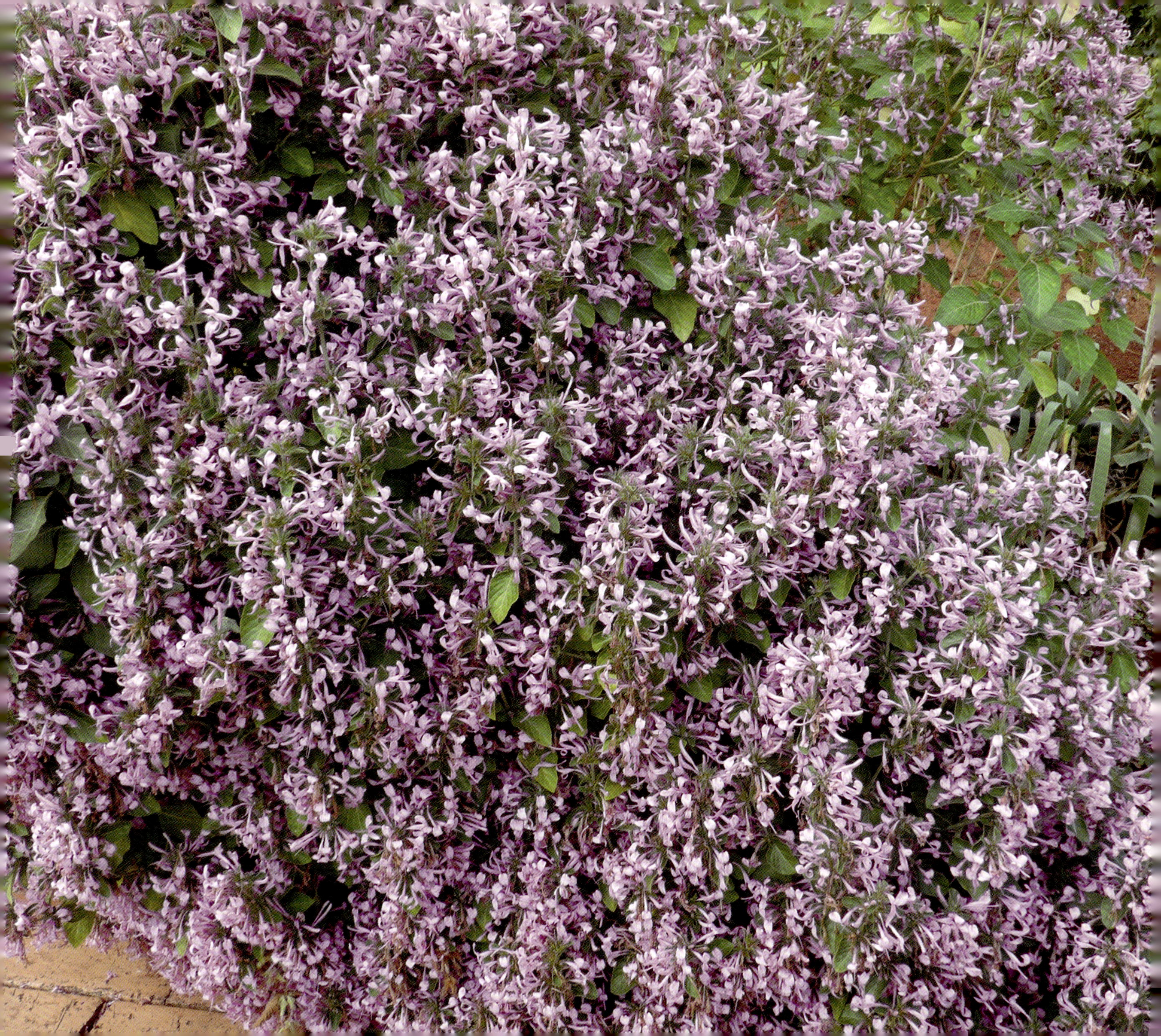

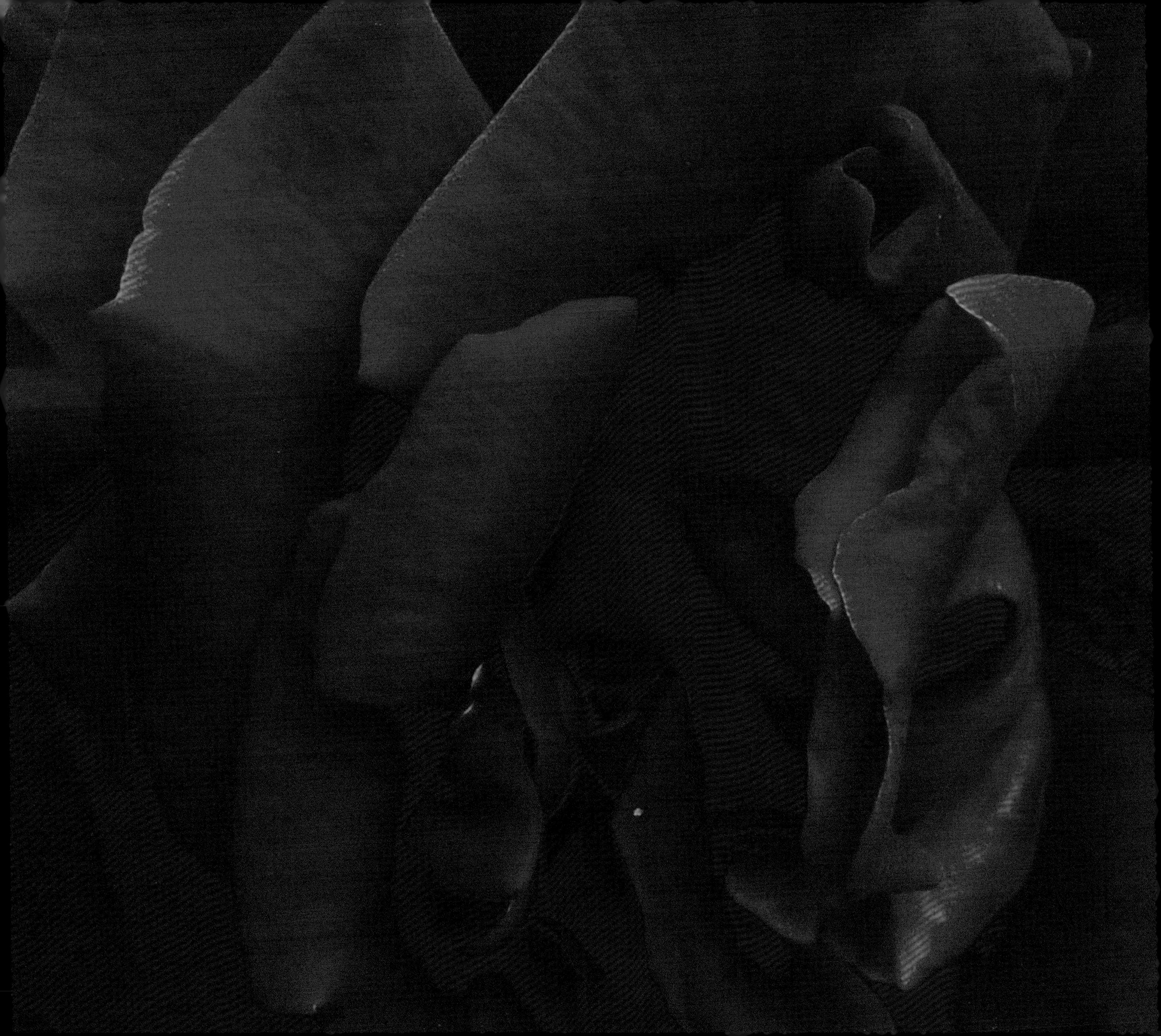

ABOVE: *This picture was taken of the rose garden in mid-April. As can be seen, there are almost as many flowers on the bushes as there are in spring.*

TOP RIGHT: *Wax tree. This small tree makes a brilliant show in early autumn with its flame-coloured leaves. It is hardy to both frost and drought.*

ABOVE RIGHT: *Yellow flax is a small shrub with light-green leaves and a mass of bright-yellow flowers in late autumn and early winter, a time when few other plants are in flower. It does well here but is not recommended for gardens where frosts are severe.*

OPPOSITE: *Roses enjoy the cool weather of autumn and flower well then, if watered.*

ABOVE: *As the leaves begin to fall in winter, wisteria adds grace and colour to the pergola. It is tolerant of severe frost and long periods of drought.*

LEFT: *Virginia creeper has been grown for generations because of its resistance to drought and cold. It will, however, do better if watered well for the first two years to encourage deep rooting. There are two kinds available - the one has tendrils and the other, which we grow, has adhesive pads by which it attaches itself to any support. Its large glossy leaves make a show for nine months of the year and, in autumn, they are flamboyant – varying from gold to burnished copper to crimson.*

OPPOSITE: *The trees with golden glowing leaves behind the pond are two North American maples – Acer negundo 'Variegatum'. Their leaves are different from the typical maple leaf in that they are divided into five to seven oval leaflets 5–10 cm long, slightly and irregularly toothed. This species puts up with hotter and drier conditions than many of the other maples. Under optimum conditions the trees, which are hardy to sharp frost, will attain a height and spread of eight metres.*

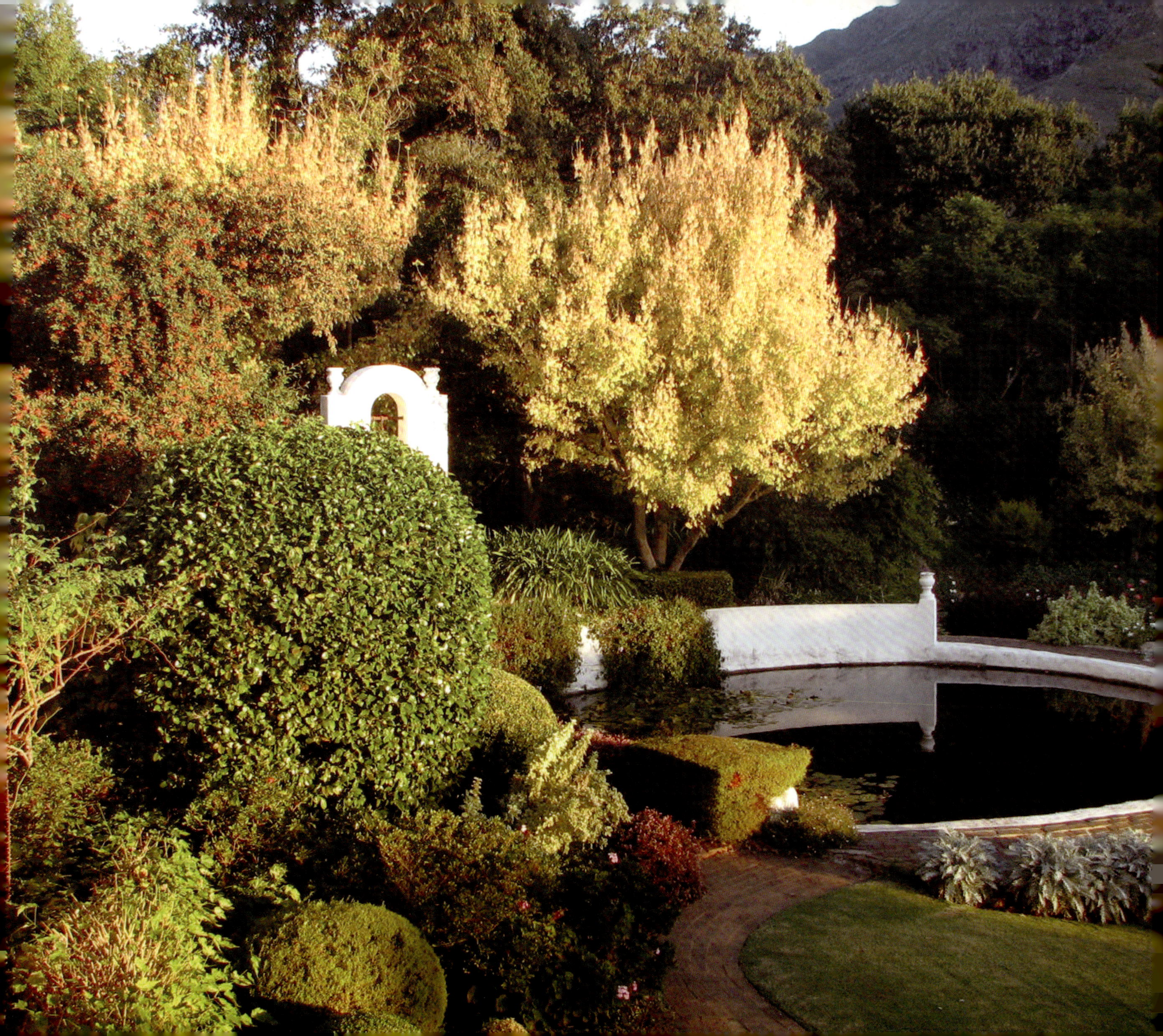

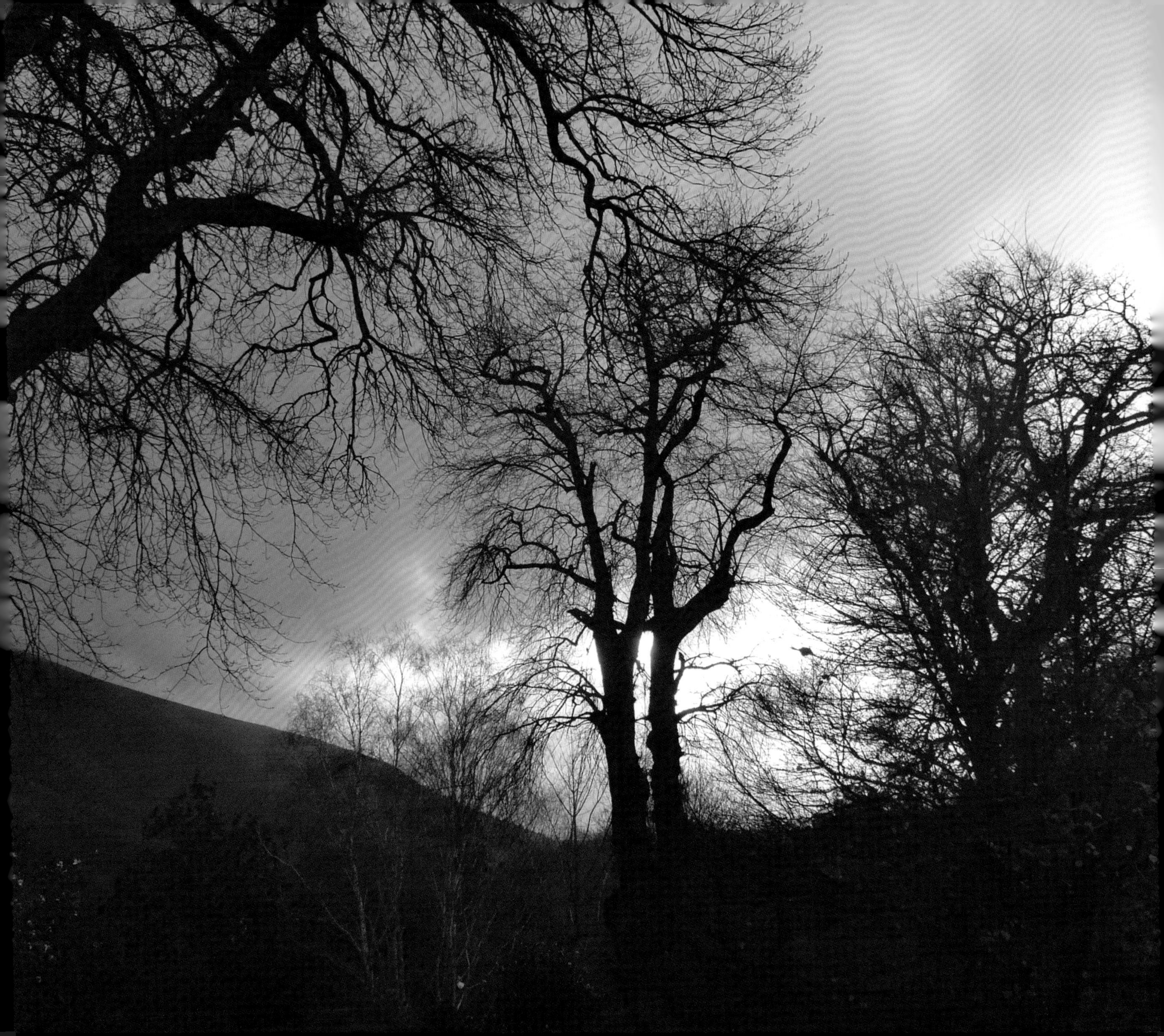

PART 11

WINTER

The clouds tumble in, dark and turbulent, powerful and assertive, as the north-west wind increases in force. It is an exhilarating wind which makes one want to fly into the sky, to be one with the dominating spirit of the coming storm. There is no thunder and lightning, as in other parts of our country, to herald the approach of a storm with a strong downflow of water. Here, the clouds drop their moisture generally slowly at first, building up in a crescendo which may continue intermittently for days. The gutters overflow and the drainage channels become blocked with falling leaves from adjacent trees. This is not a time for strolling leisurely in the garden. One rushes around unblocking the drains and wishing that the rain would cease for a while, and generally it does after three or four days, though I have known it to go on for two weeks.

The scenes from all windows of the house and through the front door remain beautiful throughout the rainy season. In front, on the mountain opposite, three waterfalls plunge down with reckless abandon. When the wind abates and, as one watches the waterfalls, they are slowly hidden from view by gossamer curtains of mist that float languorously from the north-west and then dissolve in ethereal wisps; to be obscured again and again by other drifting curtains as though the elements would keep one's interest, by continuously hiding and revealing the mountains and the waterfalls. It is an enchanting sight that gives the mountains a beauty they do not have in summer, when their outline is harshly etched against the curve of the blue sky.

At this season of the year one really appreciates the outlines of deciduous trees – each one a splendid piece of sculpture. The poplars from the plains of Lombardy in Northern Italy, so tall and stately; the oaks, old and gnarled. They have watched life go by here for 200 years. What tales they could tell? Would they remember anything at all about the people in Holland who collected the acorns brought to the Cape in sailing ships in the late 17th century? Possibly not. Thirteen generations have watched the small saplings grow through their teens to maturity, and I have had the privilege of knowing them and growing with them for the last 67 years. In that period they have almost doubled in height. What an enduring memorial to Governor Simon van der Stel, who arranged for the acorns to be brought from Holland and who insisted

OPPOSITE: *These oaks, giants of old, stand proudly erect, stately, noble and dignified. Their powerful branch structure, which ends in a lace-like pattern of twigs, forms a decorative outline against the sky whether it be blue or cloudy; or shadowed against the lime-washed walls of the old house, by day or by moonlight; or etched on the lawn, making entrancing silhouettes; or as a foreground to a flaming sunset.*

The same central tree seen in mist, sun and at sunset.

on the burghers planting them. How stark the towns and countryside would be without the progeny of those first oaks that provide us with a shady canopy during our harsh, hot summers! I do not know how many oaks there are on this five-acre property. They are of different ages, the most venerable being 200 years old or more. To my mind the oaks are more decorative in winter than in summer. In winter, when weather permits, I have lunch and tea on the stoep on the northern side of the house, admiring these towering monoliths in their naked glory.

Most of the trees in the garden are deciduous. I'm greedy; I want to have the greatest return and pleasure from each one throughout the year: the new spring growth, the summer canopy, the glorious autumnal colour and their sculptured outlines in winter.

How different in form these sculptures are. The copper beech is oval; the poplars nearby are tall and slender; then there's the elegant pattern of the branches of the Japanese maples and the ash-grey branches of the magnolias. The upturned branches of the ginkgo and the spreading crabapple standing next to it make a pleasing contrast. The chorisia from Brazil likes to be different. It sheds its leaves early in autumn, then flowers, and in early spring it begins to send out new leaves tinged bronze. It is different also in its manner of growth. It generally forms a good rounded top, but plant it too near other trees and it will grow in a contorted fashion.

The glory of the garden in the first month of winter is in the flamboyant colours of the foliage of some of the deciduous trees and shrubs. Many of these start the change of colour in late autumn, the leaves turning slowly day by day, until in mid-June right across the garden there are wonderful masses of colour.

The Japanese maples and ornamental cherries, which are also native to Japan, make a spectacular show for a long time. The leaves of both first become shades of amber to gold and then a luminous crimson hue before they drop to make splendid carpets across the lawn and paths.

The leaves of the maples are attractive in shape, elegantly arranged on the branches and decorative for nine months of the year. In addition to the type that grows into a tree there are other maples that are shrubby in growth. These last make a splendid sight in large pots. All the Japanese maples are slow-growing. There are many beautiful hybrids, some with leaves of rich ruby-red, others with leaves with a golden glow, and some with variegated leaves.

The ornamental cherries are larger in growth than the Japanese maples, but they can be pruned back lightly if they happen to outgrow their allotted space – six metres in width with a height of four to six metres. These cherries have the additional merit of producing beautiful blossoms in spring.

The snowball, which has lovely flowers in spring, is also decorative in early winter when its pretty foliage becomes a rich crimson colour. Plant near it a spice bush whose leaves turn daffodil-yellow before dropping, for a splendid early winter scene. At this time of the year the saffron leaves of the wisteria also highlight the areas where they grow, and way beyond the garden, at the foot of the mountains, tall poplars along the river keep their yellow leaves for a long time, making a pleasing backdrop to the garden.

When the trees with leaves which turn crimson are almost bare, one is delighted by the leaves of the ginkgo. These turn pure gold and, outlined against a deep blue sky, make a really spectacular show. The ginkgo belongs to the age of fossils. It is the sole survivor of a family of trees that flourished in prehistoric times. Ginkgo is sometimes called the maidenhair tree as the leaves resemble those of the maidenhair fern. The old syringa on the fringe of the garden makes a charming picture next when its leaves change to custard-yellow, and finally the golden elm sheds its leaves. In two months the garden has changed completely. Gone are millions and millions of leaves and one can now delight in the forms of the trees, their many shapes and the tracery of their branches.

Of the deciduous trees, only the magnolias flower in winter. As there are many different magnolias, one has to know the botanical name in order to be sure of acquiring the right plant. This is surely *Magnolia soulangeana*. I was so charmed by its lovely, large, pink-mauve flowers carried proudly erect on ash-grey branches that I planted eight of them in a line extending across the garden from north to south. In winter I look down from the high stoep of the house on to magnolia flowers right across the garden. They make an impressive scene.

A garden really needs evergreen as well as deciduous plants. The evergreen plants that highlight the garden at Old Nectar in winter are camellias. I planted a couple in my first year here and have continued to plant them ever since. The collection, which now numbers 40, includes the autumn-flowering types, *Camellia sasanqua*, as well as the winter-flowering type, *Camellia japonica*. One can grow them as large shrubs or trim out some of the bottom growth to create small shade trees. The glossy leaves show up well against the deciduous trees and shrubs, and are a grand background to their exquisitely shaped flowers of white and palest pink through rose to a rich, deep crimson.

These plants produce masses of buds huddled together and, as a lower bud opens, it pushes off the already-open flower, so throughout the winter there are carpets of flowers on the ground in the different areas where the camellias grow. If my garden was so small that there was space for only one large shrub or small tree, it would be a camellia, and, if I could return to this world as a flower, it would be as a camellia. Our jet-black Labrador, Bella-bella, walks around almost every day with a camellia in her mouth. She too, it seems, loves these flowers. Whilst admiring the beauty of the camellias I think about the most popular beverage consumed all over the world – tea. The plant from which tea leaves come is also a camellia. Camellias are native to the Far East.

A climber that flowers in late winter and early spring with flowers of clear yellow is the Carolina jasmine. It is a charming evergreen that grows around a pillar and also decorates a fence with its neat, glossy, dark-green leaves. It flowers when most of the climbers in the pergola are dormant and makes a lively show. I am not fond of the colour orange but do appreciate the cheerful show that golden shower makes along the pergola where it climbs a fence and up a pillar. It starts flowering in late autumn and continues until the middle of July – a period here that is often misty and one therefore appreciates some vibrant colour to brighten the garden. When it is not in flower, its glossy leaves remain decorative. We trim it back when it spreads too far and wide. Another cheerful evergreen plant that bears yellow flowers in winter is a jasmine (*Jasminum primulinum*). It is suitable only for the large garden as it is too vigorous in growth for a small area. It will grow under the harshest of conditions – frost, drought and poor soil. I planted it to hide unsightly areas. It always has a pleasing verdant appearance even when entirely neglected. It does need trimming once a year.

When the oak trees were smaller and the flower beds had more sun, we planted masses of pansies, ranunculi, anemone and indigenous bulbs for late-winter and early-spring colour, but the tall oaks now cast their shade far and wide, greatly limiting what I can grow by way of annuals, perennials and bulbs.

One of the earliest of the bulbous plants to emerge is the charming little snowflake with its nodding, chalice-shaped white flowers flecked with bright green. It's a joyous little plant all too willing to grow – no matter what! Every three years we weed it out as it spreads far and wide in my shady garden. Soon after the snowflakes appear, the flowers of hellebore start opening. This is a delightful, low-growing, winter-flowering perennial. About 20 years ago I was given the first plants by an enthusiastic gardening friend who has long since departed this life. What a fine memorial her plants are, as they have multiplied wonderfully and I set out the progeny in different shady areas.

Seeds of forget-me-not which I brought back from a visit to Alaska 12 years ago germinated well and now in late winter make patches of blue between the dormant roses along the pergola. Interspersed with them are the fern-like leaves of columbines and hellebores, which also seed themselves, making patterns of colour in the shady areas. How kind of them to spread their charm and beauty with no assistance from me.

Passing by plants in my garden from other countries I have visited makes walking and busying myself in the garden so much more interesting as I recall my travels in their homelands. In Alaska, I encountered for the first time the dogs that compete in the famous Iditarod 1,000-mile race in that country, during March, before the ice melts. A couple of years after my visit, the time taken by the winning team was only ten days. Huskies are not large dogs. It's their thick winter coats that make them appear so. They weigh only 20–30 kg. I find it difficult to believe that such small animals can cover 1,000 miles pulling a sledge, in so short a time and under such gruelling conditions. The humble little forget-me-not, the seeds of which I bought in Alaska, reminds me of those indomitable dogs ready to do their best.

In late winter, here, there and everywhere, nasturtiums frolic around, showing off their pretty leaves and gaily-coloured flowers. I love them for their boundless energy and determination to grow – up and down banks and over whatever neighbouring plants they can scramble, but in due course, and with a heavy heart, I cut them back so that the plants they've hidden can display their beauty too.

Here and there are little groups of daffodils – a memorial to my dearly beloved late husband. He planted the daffodils more than 25 years ago. We had, before then, tried to grow them, but each year most of them fed the moles. He tried putting the bulbs in netting-wire cages sunk into the earth – with better results. Then someone told him that the secret was to fill the soil beneath and around the bulbs with broken glass. This worked and now, more than two decades later, their progeny produce flowers each winter.

The golden berries and the last of the leaves of the syringa sparkle in the sunlight and add lustre to the low clouds on a dull winter's day when all the surrounding plants have already lost their leaves. I have never found seedlings around any of the three syringas on the fringe of the garden and derive great joy from their handsome form, their fragrant flowers and their attractive leaves in the other seasons.

I was astonished and delighted one winter's day when an overseas visitor, standing next to me and looking down on the rose garden from the front stoep, remarked, 'How attractive your rose garden is!' We had just finished the pruning and there were therefore no flowers or leaves on the plants. Its circular outline, the wedge-shaped beds and the brick paths separating them were cleanly and clearly delineated. It is a pleasing picture against its background of evergreen trees. I had always thought so, but nobody had said that before. This is where formal design and planting win over an informal style. The outline, rather than the plants alone, creates the scene.

The pruning of the roses, which we start during the last week of July and finish by mid-August, is one of the pleasant tasks of winter. My staff love trimming plants back (and so do I). We start by cutting them all back by a third. I explain to them that rose plants are like people inasmuch as they come in different sizes and that, after we have finished pruning, the taller ones should still be taller than the short ones. Next, we remove old stems that lack new growth or appear unhealthy at or near the base. We keep only five or six of the main stems. Then we remove spindly growth.

We always cut the stems just above a growth point – easily visible when the plants have leaves – in the axils of the leaves. When the plants are dormant, the growth points are often no more than faint marks on the stem, or minute protuberances. To ensure a bush of good shape, we cut where the growth will be in an outside direction rather than facing across the centre of the bush. The health and vigour of the plant will not be adversely affected if one makes the cut elsewhere.

The pruning of climbers is different. If their main canes are too long for their allotted space in the garden, shorten them a little, and, if there are more than four to six main canes, cut the excess out at the base, and then shorten the twiggy side-growth to within a thumb-length of the stem from which such twigs emerge.

Our next task is to spray them with an insecticide that will combat scale insects but not harm other insects. Scale insects are more bothersome in this garden than elsewhere because of the shade. Some of the roses are in shade for half the day. Scale insects show up as tiny scabs on the main stems or the back of the leaves, first mainly near the base of the plant, and, if allowed to develop further, they will weaken and eventually kill the rose. We use oleum or lime sulphur according to directions on the container. We also fertilise the plants soon after pruning using either the mixture 3:1:5 or 8:1:5. The figures printed on bags of fertiliser indicate the proportions of different nutrients. The first figure refers to nitrogen, the second to phosphorus and the third to potash. Fertilising is a very simple task. We simply scatter the granules around the base of each rose fairly near, but not touching, the main growth, using a handful for two plants.

Rain, mist or shine, the garden at Old Nectar is beautiful all winter through.

ABOVE: *Arums, known abroad as calla lilies, were for a long time favourite flowers for arrangements. In winter, in the south-western Cape, they appear in their millions covering vast hectares of farmland. They grow with exuberance in our gardens too and would take over entirely if we did not weed them out. I try to confine them to the streambed. These are handsome flowers for any garden. All they need is to be kept watered during the weeks before and during flowering.*

ABOVE LEFT: *This aloe hugs the very dry steep bank at the back of the house. It, and the white rose in the background planted 60 years ago, are beyond all the watering systems and therefore receive no water during our long, hot, dry summers. However, each year, towards the end of winter, the rose carries its crown of flowers proudly aloft.*

LEFT: *Alyssum is one of the plants that emerge without any encouragement. They brighten the garden when the trees are bare of leaves and the scene is a little austere. There are shades of pink, mauve and purple available, but we have only the white to add sparkle to the pools of shade. It is often referred to as 'sweet' alyssum because of the honey-like scent the flowers give off when they first appear. It enjoys sun rather than shade but will perform in half-hearted fashion in shady places. They flower on and off through much of the year.*

Camellias embellish many areas of the garden at Old Nectar during autumn and winter. They enjoy the rain and cloudy atmosphere we have during their flowering season and the acidity of the soil near and under the old oaks. They do better in filtered shade than in full sun. The main reason for planting so many of them is that the different types flower for such a long period from May to October and their enchanting flowers show up so well against their lustrous dark-green leaves. Camellias tolerate considerable frost, provided they are well watered when forming flowers from late summer to the end of winter and provided also that they are growing in a shady place.

ABOVE: *Carolina jasmine. This evergreen plant has willowy stems that can be trained along a fence or wall or up a pillar. In late winter and early spring it produces cascades of fragrant, golden, funnel-shaped flowers up to 3 cm long. All parts of this plant are said to be poisonous, but in the 25 years it has been growing in my garden there have been no unpleasant incidents. It stands moderate frost but not long periods with little water. Should it become top-heavy, trim some of the growth immediately after flowering is over.*

LEFT: *The copper beech is a large and handsome tree, slow in growth but decorative from its earliest years. In summer the deep copper leaves form a focal point in the garden and in winter they glow with a myriad subtle colours for two to three weeks before they fall. It does best where winters are cool to cold and in a high-rainfall area.*

OPPOSITE PAGE

TOP LEFT: *The finely serrated leaves of the ornamental cherry are lovely at any time but quite outstanding in winter when they assume a wide range of tones from amber to gold, rose and russet-red before dropping to decorate the ground below.*

BOTTOM LEFT: *Daffodils, the harbinger of spring in the northern hemisphere, here make their appearance in winter. Their cheerful yellow colour shines out on the many cloudy days we have at this time of the year. It belongs to the narcissus group of plants of which there are many types; all of them like cool-to-cold winters for their best development.*

RIGHT: *Golden shower has dark-green glossy leaves that make a handsome screen throughout the year. Here the flowers climbing up a pergola pillar add vibrant colour in winter. This climber grows and flowers well where winters are not severe. It should be watered in autumn and winter to encourage good flowering.*

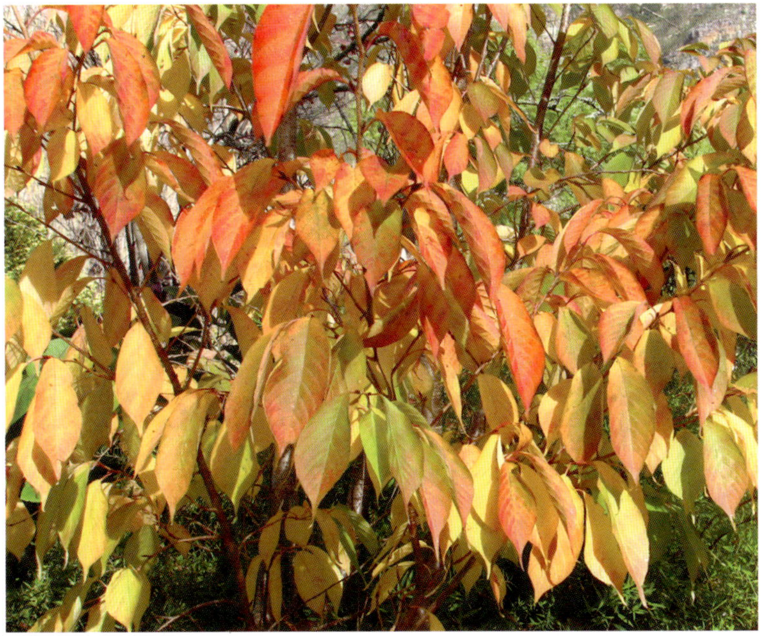

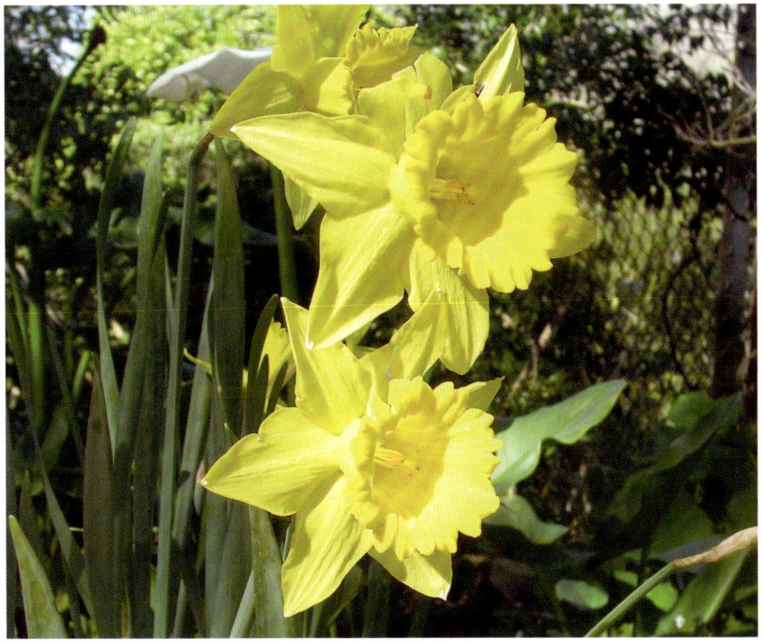

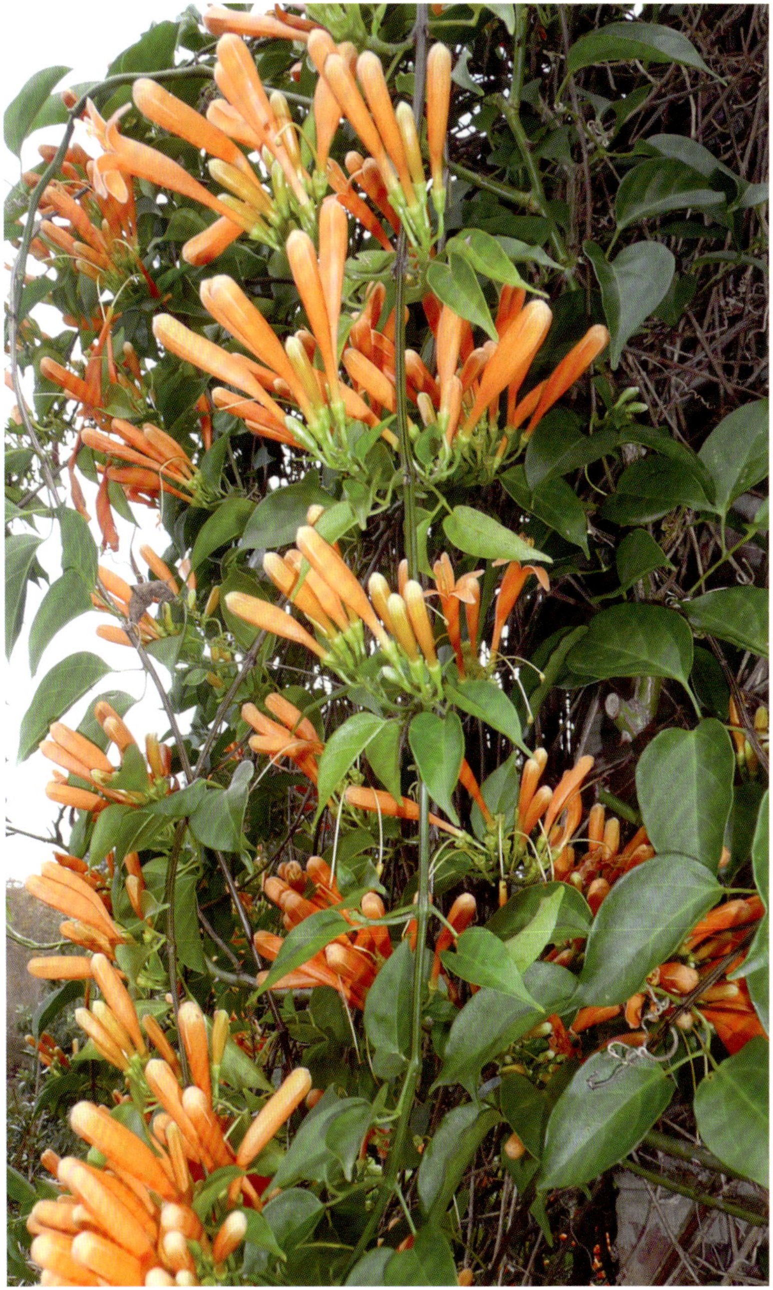

ABOVE: *Hellebore is the name of one of the most decorative of the perennial ground-cover plants that do well in shade. It is native to the lower Italian Alps and is popular in Britain, where it is known as the Christmas rose because of its time of flowering. Here it starts flowering in early winter and continues into spring – a period of three months. The flowers change in colour as they develop from ivory marked with amethyst, to pink and finally to green when the seeds form. Very often a plant has all three colours at the same time. It tolerates extreme cold but needs watering during dry periods of the year.*

LEFT: *Ginkgo makes a spectacular show of leaf colour in winter. It is not surprising that it is popular in China and Japan, to which countries it is indigenous. This is a slow-growing deciduous tree suitable for regions with cold winters, but it needs regular watering in its early life.*

The large flowers of the winter-flowering magnolia (M. soulangeana) *make a splendid show against the bare stems. It is hardy to frost but not dry conditions. Water regularly for the first four or five years.*

ABOVE: *Nandina, also known as the Japanese sacred bamboo, looks like a miniature bamboo with numerous stems growing from the ground. The leaves are attractively arranged, and in summer clusters of waxy ivory-white flowers appear, followed by crimson berries, which hang down prettily from the plant in winter. It stands long periods with little water and quite considerable frost.*

LEFT: *The fallen leaves make colourful carpets on the ground. Here we have a scattering of the leaves of cherry, ginkgo, maple and spice bush.*

OPPOSITE LEFT: *Pride of India, which bears its showy flowers in summer, becomes decorative once more in winter when its leaves assume a deep copper colour. It endures both drought and sharp frost but tends to get mildew in humid conditions.*

OPPOSITE RIGHT: *Snowball is one of my favourite large shrubs because it is a splendid sight when it flowers in spring and again in winter when the leaves slowly change to crimson before dropping. It does well in frosty gardens provided it is watered during the dry months.*

199

ABOVE: *Because of the delightful shape of the leaves and their elegant arrangement on the stems, maples add to the beauty of the garden for much of the year. They need good soil, preferably slightly acid, and some shade, either on the south side of a building or else under large trees. They do not thrive under warm or dry conditions.*

OPPOSITE: *This picture shows up the contrast in shades of colour provided by leaves and leafless stems and branches. A trimmed, round golden conifer is backed by the silver leaves of a gazania. To the right are the deep bronze leaves of the ground cover named polygonum. The bare silvery stems of the snowball bush show up against the handsome outline of the copper beech with its flame-coloured winter leaves. The small burnished-bronze tree on the left is a Japanese maple. The silvery stems of the poplars lining the river bank beyond the garden highlight the scene.*

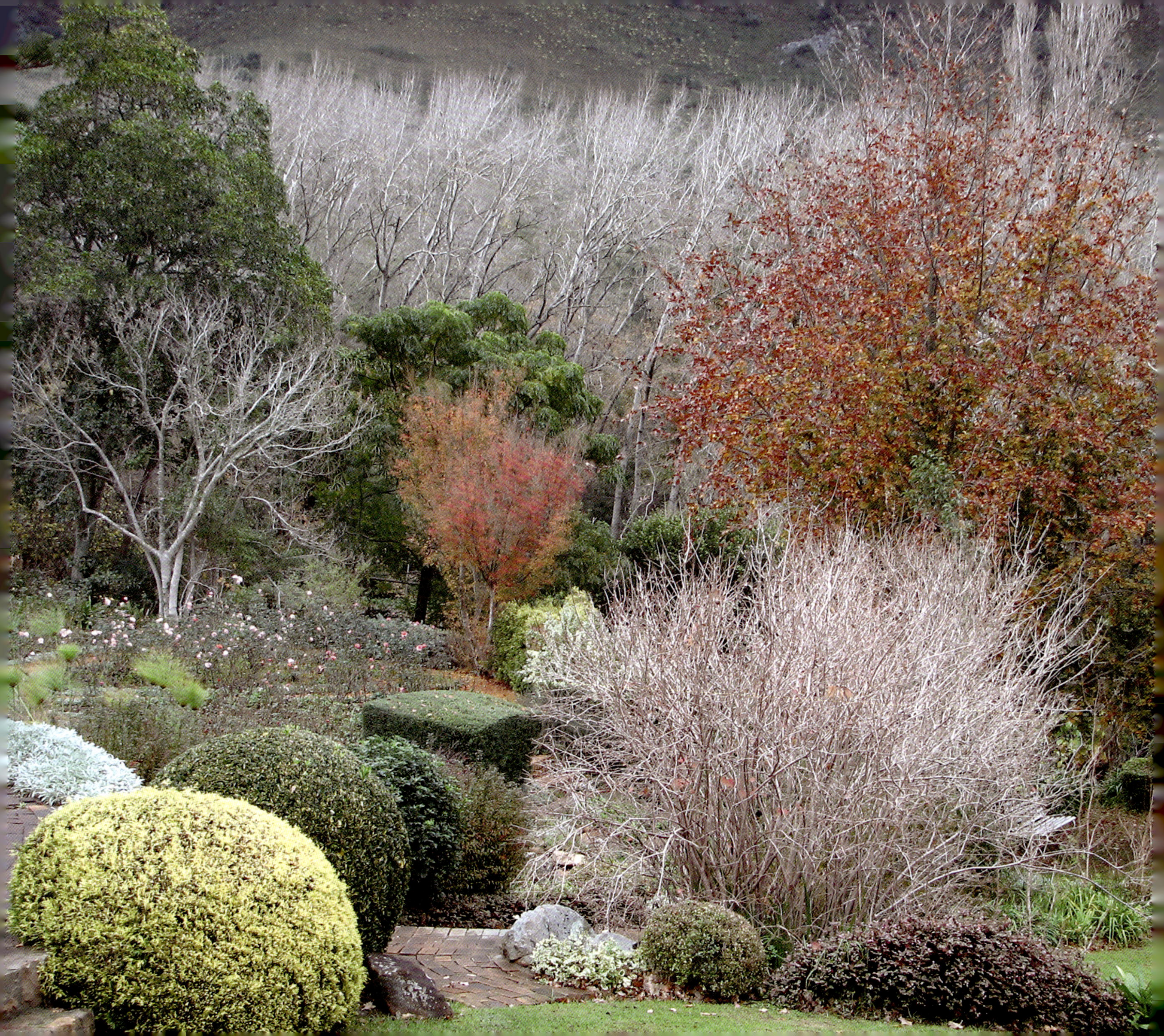

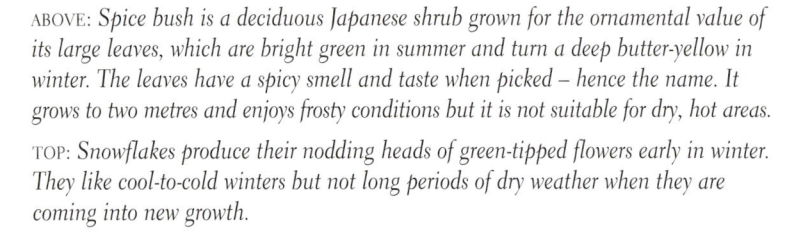

ABOVE: *Spice bush is a deciduous Japanese shrub grown for the ornamental value of its large leaves, which are bright green in summer and turn a deep butter-yellow in winter. The leaves have a spicy smell and taste when picked – hence the name. It grows to two metres and enjoys frosty conditions but it is not suitable for dry, hot areas.*

TOP: *Snowflakes produce their nodding heads of green-tipped flowers early in winter. They like cool-to-cold winters but not long periods of dry weather when they are coming into new growth.*

ABOVE: *Veltheimia is an indigenous bulbous plant that grows wild in the coastal region of the eastern Cape. The large glossy leaves with a wavy margin form a decorative rosette from which arises a spike of tubular, coral-pink flowers arranged rather like those of an aloe. There is also a yellow form. It does best in shade which also protects it from frost damage. Plant in humus-rich soil.*

OPPOSITE: *Occasionally, though not very often, the setting sun, just before it disappears behind the mountain, emerges from behind a cloud to cast a glorious light over the garden. It is tantalisingly beautiful, but generally, before one can take a picture, the light vanishes.*

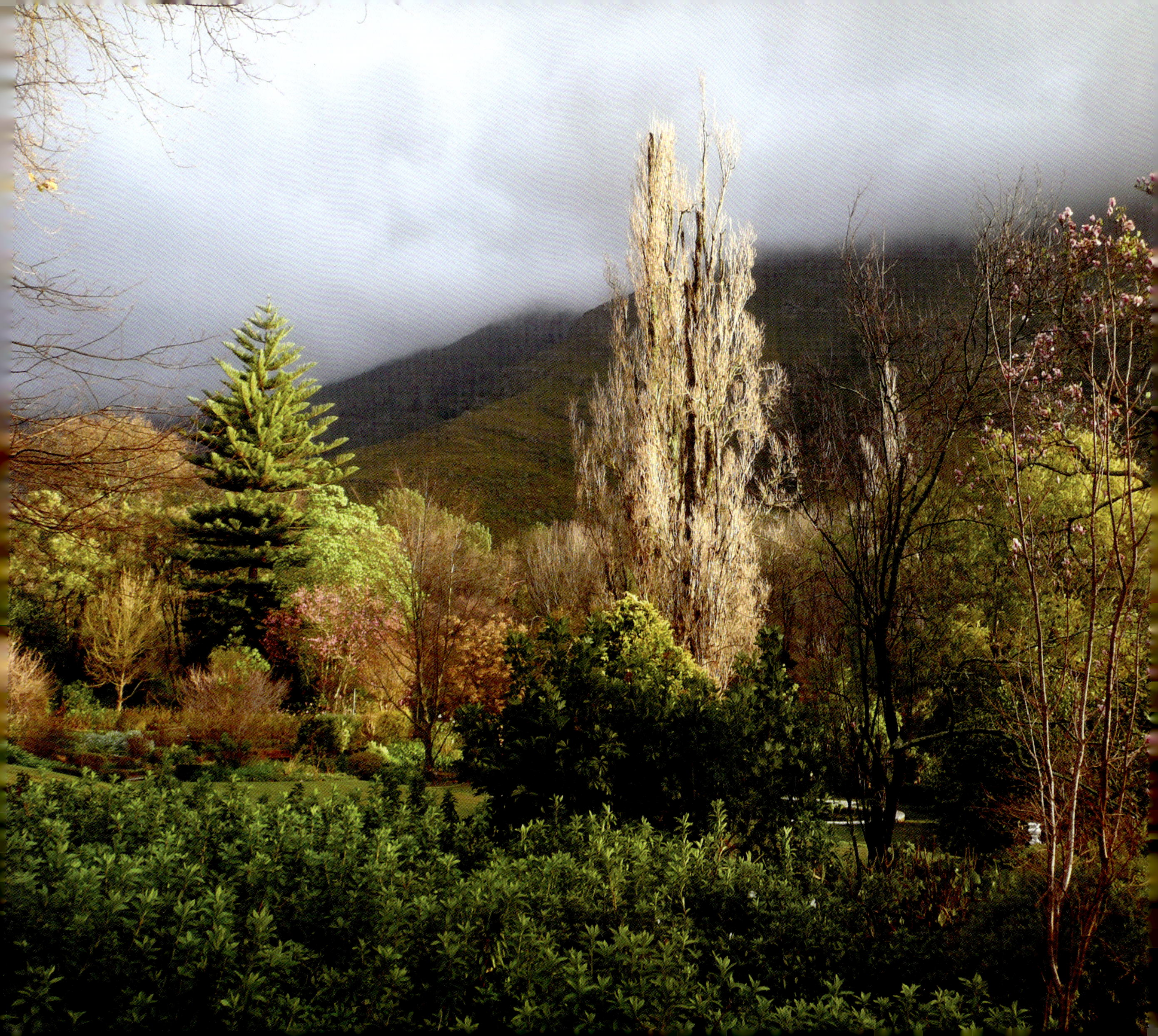

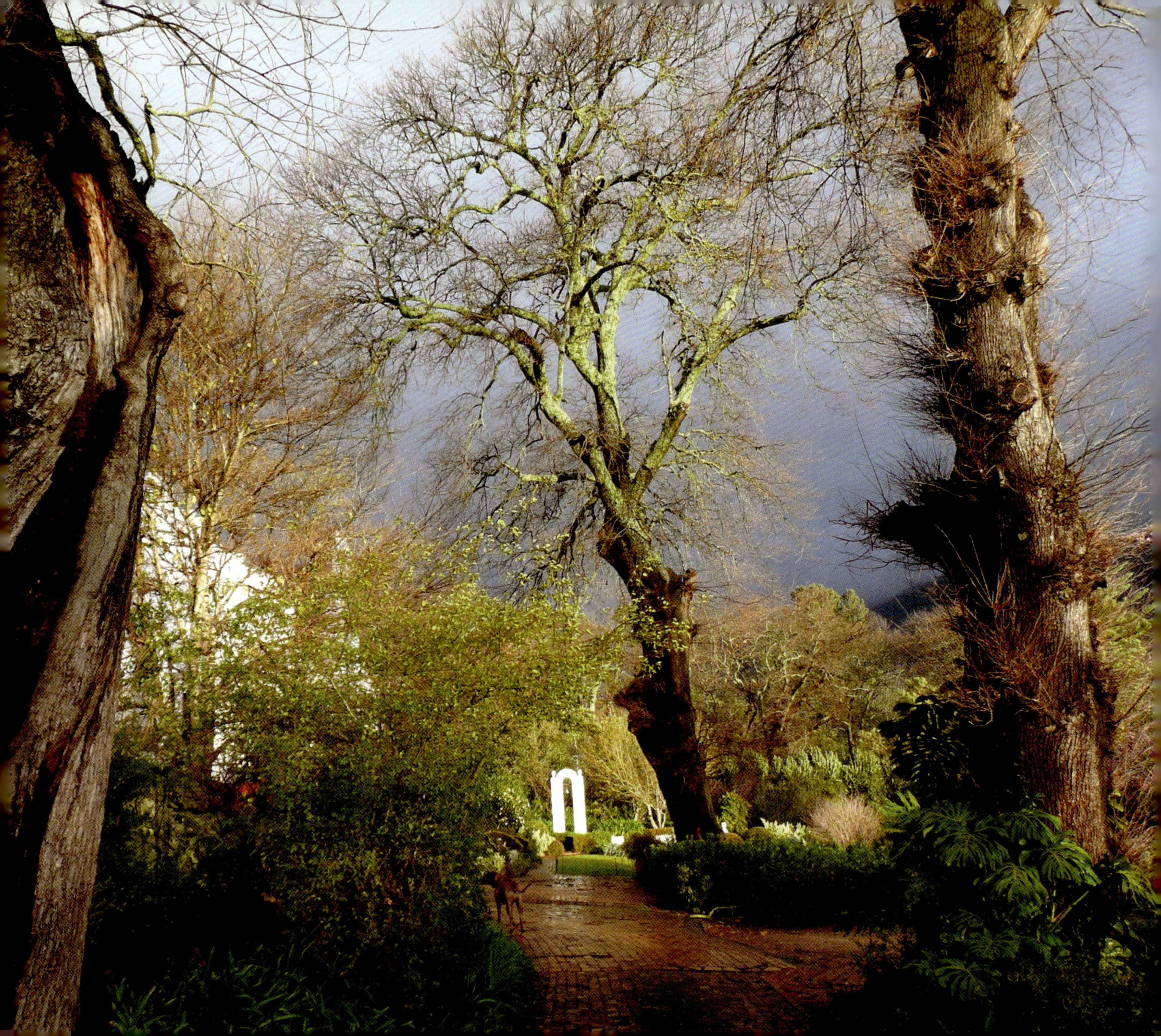

ALIEN INVADER PLANTS

Certain shrubs and trees planted 30 or more years ago, and which are described in this book, may no longer be planted as they have been declared weeds or invader plants in terms of a Conservation of Agricultural Resources Act. The list is extensive but only eight of those listed grow in the garden at Old Nectar: Australian brush cherry, cotoneaster, jacaranda, privets (golden privet excepted), lantana, pyracantha, syringa and wax tree.

The reason for the ban on their propagation is that they may proliferate and become weeds, but here they have not increased in number since planted because the climatic conditions of this area tend to inhibit the germination of their seeds.

In South Africa we have four distinct climatic zones, and plants that grow readily in warm regions of the summer-rainfall area and may indeed become weeds there, are unlikely to seed themselves in the winter-rainfall zone, nor in the vast area of the country which has a sparse rainfall, extremely hot days and severe frost. Most of the trees and shrubs mentioned above are drought and frost-resistant and therefore ideal for arid areas where few garden plants thrive. One hopes therefore that the authority concerned will take greater cognisance of these climatic differences.

Regulations and laws to limit the growing of plants which may threaten to become weeds are necessary, but the ban should be specific in its application.

In my opinion it is neither reasonable nor logical to ban the growing of plants throughout the entire country when they are likely to proliferate only in certain defined climatic zones.

OPPOSITE: *These old oaks dominate the approach up the drive to the house and garden. Their age and dignity entitle them to be sure of their importance.*

PICTURE CREDITS

The numbers below refer to the pages on which the following photographers' pictures appear. Letters identify their position on the page: t = top; b = bottom; l = left; r = right; c = centre.

Andrea du Plessis: 8, 44

Albert Potgieter: 23 r, 37 l, 40, 42 bl, 43, 50, 53, 63, 66, 68 tr, 69 tl, 69 br, 70, 73 br, 77, 84, 89, 94 bl, 97 bl, 102, 106 tl, 106 bl, 111, 115, 116 bl, 117 118, 122 r, 123 tl, 123 tr, 125, 126 r, 143, 145, 149, 156 bl, 157 l, 159, 160 bl, 161, 162 bl, 163, 170 tl, 170 tr, 172 tl, 172 bl, 174 bl, 175 tl, 175 br, 177, 178 r, 179 l, 183 tr, 185, 193 tl, 193 bl, 195 tl, 197, 201

Aileen Potgieter: 26 & 27 c, 36, 37 r, 39 bl, 39 tl, 39 tr, 42 tl, 47 tr, 55 bl, 55 r, 56, 58 tr, 58 bl, 59, 65 r, 67 tr, 74 tl, 76 r, 86 r, 96 l, 98, 99 l, 108, 110 tr, 114 tr, 122 l, 126 l, 127, 129, 131, 133, 135, 136, 144, 148 r, 152 l, 155, 156 tl, 160 tl, 172 tr, 173, 179 r, 184 l, 192 tl, 195 bl, 198 l, 202 tl

Peter van der Spuy: 4, 5, 7, 10, 18, 20, 24, 25 tr, 27 r, 29, 38, 49, 55 tl, 58 tl, 72, 73 tr, 80, 81, 83, 88 r, 90, 92, 94 tl, 114 bl, 130, 132, 134, 176

Una van der Spuy: 13, 15, 16, 17, 19, 21, 22, 23 l, 25 br, 26 l, 28, 30, 32, 33, 34, 35, 39 br, 41, 42 tr, 46, 47 br, 47 tl, 48, 51, 52, 54, 57, 60, 62, 64, 65 l, 67 tl, 67 b, 68 l, 68 br, 69 tr, 74 r, 74bl, 75, 76 l, 78, 85, 86 l, 87, 88 l, 93, 94 tr, 94 br, 95, 96 r, 97 r, 97 tl, 99 r, 100, 101, 106 tr, 109, 110 l, 110 br, 112, 113, 114 tl, 116 tl, 116 tr, 119, 120, 121, 123 br, 124, 128, 138, 140, 142, 146, 147, 148 l, 150, 151, 152 r, 153, 154, 156 tr, 157 r, 158, 162 tl, 162 tr, 164, 166, 168, 170 br, 174 tl, 174 tr, 175 tr, 178 l, 180, 181, 182, 183 l, 183 br, 184 r, 186, 188, 192 bl, 192 tr, 193 tr, 193 br, 194, 195 r, 196, 198 r, 199, 200, 202 bl, 202 r, 203

INDEX
Page numbers in italics refer to photographs

Abelia, golden	*Abelia x grandiflora* 'Francis Mason'	33, 80, *85*, 141
Abutilon	*Abutilon x hybridum* 'Variegatum'	*21, 48, 84*
Agapanthus	*Agapanthus praecox*	32, 61, *63, 76*, 137, 141, *142*
Ageratum (giant)	*Eupatorium fulgens*	27, *38*, 107, *116*
Aloe	*Aloe arborescens*	*192*
Alyssum	*Lobularia maritima*	*192*
American maple	*Acer negundo* 'Variegatum'	29, *30*, 32
Aristolochia	*Aristolochia littoralis*	141, *143*
Arum	*Zantedeschia aethiopica*	137, *192*
Australian brush cherry	*Syzygium paniculatum*	*143*
Australian frangipani	*Hymenosporum flavum*	14, 15, *16, 30, 106*, 107
Australian myrtle	*Syzygium paniculatum*	*143*, 167, *170*
Azalea	*Rhododendron* cultivars	24, 25, 26, 27, 60, 62, 64, 72, 74, 94, 104, *106, 108*, 109
Banksia rose	*Rosa banksiae* 'Lutea'	*88*, 107
Begonia	*Begonia semperflorens*	139, *144*
Belladonna lily	*Amaryllis belladonna*	165, 167, *170*
Berberis	*Berberis thunbergii*	*22*, 32, *85*
	B. thunbergii 'Rose Glow'	*161*
Bignonia	*Bignonia cherere* (*Distictis buccinatoria*)	139
Bignonia mauve	*Clytostoma callistegioides*	*155*
Birch, silver	*Betula pendula*	67, 75, *172*
Black spot on roses		105
Bluebell	*Hyacinthoides hispanica*	82, 91, *98*, 107, *108*
Bougainvillea	*Bougainvillea glabra* hybrids	*93*
Bower vine	*Pandorea jasminioides*	139, *145*
Brunfelsia	*Brunfelsia pauciflora* 'Eximia'	*78*, 109, *109*
Bulbine	*Bulbine frutescens*	*110*
California redwood	*Sequoia sempervirens*	169
Camellia	*Camellia japonica*	28, 45, *57, 69, 70, 75, 89, 92, 96, 97*
	Camellia sasanqua	*166, 169, 170*, 190
Campsis	*Campsis grandiflora*	68
Canary creeper	*Senecio tamoides*	171, *172*
Canna	*Canna* hybrid cultivars	80-1, *85, 86*
Cantua	*Cantua buxifolia*	*110*
Cape may	*Spiraea cantoniensis*	33, *38*, 107, *110*, 112
Carolina jasmine	*Gelsemium sempervirens*	*47*, 190, *194*
Cerastium	*Cerastium tomentosum*	*112*
Cherry	*Prunus serrulata* cultivars	*65*, 195
Cherry	*Prunus serrulata* 'Kanzan'	*53*, 104, *111*
Chinese redwood	*Sequoia glyptostroboides*	169
Chinese trumpet climber	*Campsis grandiflora*	139, *146*
Choisya	*Choisya ternata*	*112*
Chorisia	*Chorisia speciosa*	169, 171, *172, 173*, 189
Clematis	*Clematis* hybrid cultivars	54, *55, 56*, 109, *113*
Clematis	*Clematis montana*	*55*, 109, *113*
Clematis	*Clematis paniculata*	141
Columbine	*Aquilegia vulgaris* hybrids	23, *113*, 190
Combretum	*Combretum fruticosum*	141, *147, 168*, 171
Copper beech	*Fagus sylvatica* 'Purpurea'	14, *15*, 107, 137, 141, 189, *194*, 201
Coprosma	*Coprosma repens* 'Variegata'	*37*
Cotoneaster	*Cotoneaster franchetii*	*147*, 169, *174*
Crabapple	*Malus* hybrid cultivar	*52, 56*, 61, *65*, 114, *148*, 189
Crassula	*Crassula falcata*	165, 167
	Crassula multicava	167
Creeping Jenny	*Lysimachia nummularia* 'Aurea'	*21*
Crinum	*Crinum bulbispermum*	*114*
	Crinum macowanii	137, *148*
Crocosmia	*Crocosmia aurea*	167, *174*
Daffodil	*Narcissus* hybrid cultivar	191, *195*
Day lily	*Hemerocallis* hybrid cultivar	32, *115*
Dusty miller	*Senecio cineraria* 'Silver Dust'	*19, 34, 38*, 80, *85*, 141
Elderberry	*Sambucus nigra* 'Marginata'	32
Elm, golden	*Ulmus carpinifolia* 'Aurea'	189
Erigeron	*Erigeron karvinskianus*	*20*, 114
Firewheel tree	*Stenocarpus sinuatus*	141, *149*
Forget-me-not	*Myosotis alpestris*	107, 190
Fungus diseases		105, 169
Gazania	*Gazania rigens* var. *leucolaena*	32, 80, 141, *201*
Geranium	*Geranium incanum*	*20*, 116
Giant ageratum	*Eupatorium fulgens*	27, *38*, 107, *116*
Ginkgo	*Ginkgo biloba*	61, *63, 68*, 189, *196, 198*
Golden abelia	*Abelia x grandiflora* 'Francis Mason'	33, 80, *85*, 141
Golden conifer	*Chamaecyparis* hybrid cultivar	*17*, 141, *201*
Golden elder	*Sambucus nigra* 'Marginata'	34
Golden privet	*Ligustrum ovalifolium* 'Aureum'	*17, 19, 21, 22, 23*, 80, *85*, 141

Common name	Botanical name	Pages
Golden robinia	Robinia pseudoacacia 'Aurea'	*84*, 137, 141, 169
Golden shower	Pyrostegia venusta	45, *48*, 190, *195*
Guinea gold vine	Hibbertia scandens	139, *150*
Gunnera	Gunnera manicata	15, *22*, 107
Hawthorn	Crataegus phaenopyrum	*174*
Hellebore	Helleborus orientalis	61, *64*, 82, 190, *196*
Hibbertia	Hibbertia scandens	150
Hibiscus	Hibiscus rosa-sinensis	139, *151*
Holly, variegated	Ilex aquifolium hybrid cultivar	*82*, 88
Honeysuckle	Lonicera periclymenum	*116*
Honeysuckle, wild	Tecomaria capensis	141, 165, *175*
Horse chestnut	Aesculus hippocastanum	107, *117*
Hydrangea	Hydrangea hortensia cultivars	61, *69*, *76*, *138*, 139, 171, *175*
Hymenosporum	Hymenosporum flavum	*14*, 109
Impatiens	Impatiens hybrid cultivar	82, *95*, 139, *152*
Indian hawthorn	Raphiolepis x Delacourii	*119*
Iris	Iris hybrid cultivar	*62*, 118
Iris	Iris japonica	*119*
Jacaranda	Jacaranda mimosifolia	*137*, 152
Japanese anemone	Anemone hupehensis	61, *69*, 167, *175*
Japanese cherry	Prunus serrulata	*37*, *53*, 61, *66*, 104
Japanese maple	Acer japonicum	91, 104, 189, *201*
	Acer palmatum	*37*, 91, *94*, 104
	Acer palmatum 'Atropurpureum'	90, 141, 169, 189, *200*
	Acer palmatum 'Dissectum Atropurpureum'	*60*, *94*, 95
Japanese sacred bamboo	Nandina domestica	*198*
Jasmine	Jasminum polyanthum	15, 45, *47*, 107, 119
Jasmine (winter)	Jasminum primulinum	*190*
Justicia	Justicia carnea	*96*, 139, *153*
Kanzan (cherry)	Prunus serrulata 'Kanzan'	*111*
Kapok tree	Chorisia speciosa	*171*
Lamb's ear	Stachys byzantina	*22*
Lamium	Lamium maculatum	*27*
Lantana	Lantana camara	137, *154*
Lavender	Lavendula angustifolia	15, *78*
Lemon balm	Melissa officinalis	15, *78*
Leucospermum	Leucospermum reflexum	*122*
Liquidambar	Liquidambar styraciflua	79, 104, 169, *177*
Lombardy poplar	Populus nigra 'Italica'	14, *15*, 167, 169, *178*, 187
Lotus, trailing	Lotus berthelotii	*21*
Luculia	Luculia gratissima	82, 91, *99*, 171, *178*
Magnolia	Magnolia liliiflora	*120*
Magnolia	Magnolia soulangeana	*37*, *77*, 189, *197*
	Magnolia stellata	*121*
Malvaviscus	Malvaviscus arboreus	139, *154*
Maple, American	Acer negundo 'Variegatum'	29, *30*, *32*, *185*
Maple, Japanese	Acer japonicum	91, 104, 189, *201*
	Acer palmatum	*37*, 91, *94*, 104
	Acer palmatum 'Atropupureum'	90, 141, 169, 189, *200*
	Acer palmatum 'Dissectum Atropurpureum'	*60*, *94*, 95
March lily	Amaryllis belladonna	*170*
Mauve bignonia	Clytostoma callistegioides	*155*
Mexican blood trumpet	Distictis buccinatoria	*47*, 139, *156*
Mexican orange blossom	Choisya ternata	*107*
Mildew		105, 160, 198
Mock orange	Philadelphus coronarius	107, *126*
Moonflower	Brugmansia x candida	79, 139, *156*
	Brugmansia x insignis	*157*
	Brugmansia x sanguinea	*156*
Moses-in-the-bulrushes	Tradescantia andersonia hybrid	*86*, 126
Murraya	Murraya paniculata	*123*
Nandina	Nandina domestica	*34*, 198
Nasturtium	Tropaeolum majus	*33*, 109, 123, 191
Nerina	Nerine sarniensis	*167*
New Zealand clematis	Clematis paniculata	*158*
Norfolk Island pine	Araucaria heterophylla	16, *30*, *32*, 33, 34
Oak	Quercus robur	91, *186*, *187*, *188*
Ochna	Ochna serrulata	*123*
Orange River lily	Crinum bulbispermum	*114*
Papyrus	Cyperus papyrus	*15*
Paulownia	Paulownia tomentosa	109, *157*
Peach	Prunus persica cultivar	*52*, *63*, *125*
Pelargonium	Pelargonium cultivar	*26*, 81
Periwinkle	Vinca major	*19*
Persimmon	Diospyros kaki	169, *179*
Petrea	Petrea volubilis	79, *80*, 109, *124*
Philadelphus	Philadelphus caronarius	15, 107, *126*
Pieris	Pieris formosa cultivar	*68*, *127*
Pineapple flower	Eucomis autumnalis	*32*, 139, *159*
Plectranthus	Plectranthus ecklonii	165, *179*
Plectranthus (trailing)	Plectranthus madagascariensis	*95*
Plumbago	Plumbago auriculata	33, *34*, 141, *160*, 165, *180*
Polygonum	Polygonum capitatum	19, *23*, *201*
Pride of de Kaap	Bauhinia galpinii	*141*

Pride of India	*Lagerstroemia indica*	67, *141*, *160*, 171, *199*
Privet	*Ligustrum ibota*	34, *126*
Prunus	*Prunus cerasifera* 'Nigra'	27, 31, *38*, *90*, *102*, *126*
Pyracantha	*Pyracantha angustifolia*	169, *180*
Rhododendron	*Rhododendron* hybrid cultivar	81, *87*, *94*, 109, *128*
Rhus	*Rhus succedanea*	183
Ribbon bush	*Hypoestes aristata*	169, *181*
Robinia	*Robinia pseudoacacia* hybrid cultivar	81, *84*, 137, 141, 169
Rocket pincushion	*Leucospermum reflexum*	*122*
Rose	*Rosa* cultivars	30-43, *45*, 46, *48-51*, *58*, *73*, *80*, 81, *85*, *88*, *90*, *97*, *129*, *130*, *131*, *136*, *140*, *161*, *182*, *183*, *201*
Rose diseases		105, 169
Rose pruning		105, 141, 191
Rosemary	*Rosmarinus officinalis*	15
Rust		105, 169
Scale insect		191
Shasta daisy	*Leucanthemum superbum*	137, *162*
Silver birch	*Betula pendula*	67, *75*, *172*
Sky flower	*Thunbergia grandiflora*	45, 109, *162*
Snowball	*Viburnum opulus*	22, *53*, 61, 109, *132*, 189, *199*, 201
Snowflake	*Leucojum aestivum*	61, 190, *202*
Snow-in-summer	*Cerastium tomentosum*	31, *112*
Sparaxis	*Sparaxis grandiflora*	104
Spice bush	*Lindera benzoin*	61, *67*, *198*, *202*
Spiraea (see Cape may)	*Spiraea cantoniensis*	33, *38*, 107, *110*, 112
Spring magnolia	*Magnolia liliiflora*	120
Spurflower	*Plectranthus ecklonii*	165, *179*
Star jasmine	*Trachelospermum jasminoides*	59, *139*
Star magnolia	*Magnolia stellata*	121
Syringa	*Melia azedarach*	91, *133*, 189, 191
Thunbergia (sky flower)	*Thunbergia grandiflora*	109, *162*
Valerian	*Centranthus ruber*	*134*
Variegated maple	*Acer negundo* 'Variegatum'	14, *185*
Veltheimia	*Veltheimia bracteata*	202
Viburnum (snow ball)	*Viburnum opulus*	22, *53*, 61, 104, 109, *132*, 189, *199*, 201
Virginia creeper	*Parthenocissus tricuspidata*	81, *84*, *93*, 171, *184*
Water lily	*Nymphaea* cultivar	18, *163*
Wax tree	*Rhus succedanea*	183
Willow	*Salix babylonica*	79
Wisteria	*Wisteria sinensis*	45, *46*, 107, *184*
Yellow flax	*Reinwardtia indica*	183
Yellow trumpet climber	*Adenocalymma commosum*	45, *162*

First published by Jacana Media (Pty) Ltd in 2009

10 Orange Street
Sunnyside
Auckland Park 2092
South Africa
+2711 628 3200
www.jacana.co.za

© Una van der Spuy, 2009

All rights reserved. No part of this book may be reproduced or utilised in any form and by any means, electronic or mechanical, including photocopying, without permission in writing from the publisher.

ISBN 978-1-77009-756-8

Cover and text design by Jenny Young
Set in Electra and Helvetica
Printed by Imago, Malaysia
Job no. 001036

See a complete list of Jacana titles at
www.jacana.co.za